MODERN JUDAISM

VOLUME 22   NUMBER 1   FEBRUARY 2002

CONTENTS

HAUS, Jeffrey
  Liberté, Égalité, Utilité: Jewish Education and State   1
    in Nineteenth-Century France

NASH, Stanley
  Authors and Women as Antiheroes in Aharon Megged's   28
    Later Works

FINKELMAN, Yoel
  Haredi Isolation in Changing Environments: A Case Study   61
    in Yeshiva Immigration

WASSERMANN, Henry
  The *Wissenschaft des Judentums* and Protestant Theology: 83
    A Review Essay

BOOKS RECEIVED   99

CONTRIBUTORS   101

Please visit the journal's Web site at
www.mj.oupjournals.org
For more information about Oxford University Press,
please visit us at
www.oup-usa.org

Modern Judaism (ISSN 0276-1114) is published three times a year (February, May, and October) by Oxford University Press, 2001 Evans Rd., Cary, NC 27513-2009.

Oxford University Press is a department of the University of Oxford. It furthers the University's objective of excellence in research, scholarship, and education by publishing worldwide.

Subscriptions: Subscription is on a yearly basis. The annual rates are US$48 (£37 in UK and Europe) for individuals; US$121 (£82 in UK and Europe) for institutions; US$25 (£15 in UK and Europe) for students. Single issues are available for US$19 (£14 in UK and Europe) for individuals and US$51 (£35 in UK and Europe) for institutions. All prices include postage. Individual rates are only applicable when a subscription is for individual use and is not available if delivery is made to a corporate address. All subscriptions, single issue and back issue orders, changes of address, and claims for missing issues should be sent to: NORTH AMERICA: Oxford University Press, Journals Customer Service, 2001 Evans Road, Cary, NC 27513-2009, USA. Toll-free in the USA and Canada 800-852-7323 or 919-677-0977. Fax: 919-677-1714. E-mail: jnlorders@oup-usa.org; ELSEWHERE: Oxford University Press, Journals Customer Service, Great Clarendon St., Oxford OX2 6DP, UK. Tel: +44 1865 267907. Fax: +44 1865 267485. E-mail: jnl.orders@oup.co.uk

Advertising: Helen Pearson, Oxford Journals Advertising, P.O. Box 347, Abingdon, OX14 1GJ, UK. Tel/Fax: +44 1235 201904. E-mail: helen@oxfordads.com

Requests for Permissions, Reprints, and Photocopies: All rights reserved. No part of this publication may be reproduced, stored in a retrieval system, or transmitted in any form or by any means, electronic, mechanical, photocopying, recording, or otherwise, without either prior written permission of the publisher (Oxford University Press, Journals Rights and Permissions, Great Clarendon St., Oxford OX2 6DP, UK; Tel: +44 1865 267561, Fax: +44 1865 267485) or a license permitting restricted copying issued in the USA by the Copyright Clearance Center, 222 Rosewood Drive, Danvers, MA 01923, Fax: 978-750-4470; or in the UK by the Copyright Licensing Agency Ltd., 90 Tottenham Court Road, London W1P 9HE. Reprints of individual articles are available only from the authors.

Modern Judaism is indexed and abstracted in: *Abstracts of English Studies* (up to 1995), *America: History and Life, American Bibliography of Slavic & East European Studies, American Jewish Year Book, Arts & Humanities Citation Index, ATLA Religion Database, Current Contents, Historical Abstracts/Modern History, Historical Abstracts/Twentieth Century, Humanities Index, Index to Jewish Periodicals, Middle East: Abstracts & Index, MLA International Bibliography, Old Testament Abstracts, Periodica Islamica, Religion Index One, Religious & Theological Abstracts, and Research Alert.*

Modern Judaism is printed on acid-free paper that meets the minimum requirements of ANSI Standard Z39.48-1984 (Permanence of Paper).

Postmaster: Send address changes to *Modern Judaism,* Journals Customer Service Department, Oxford University Press, 2001 Evans Road, Cary, NC 27513-2009.

Copyright © 2002 Oxford University Press

Jeffrey Haus

LIBERTÉ, ÉGALITÉ, UTILITÉ: JEWISH EDUCATION AND STATE IN NINETEENTH-CENTURY FRANCE

Shortly after its formation in 1808, the Central Jewish Consistory of France—the administrative body charged with overseeing French Jewish religious activities[1]—began to solicit government permission to open specifically Jewish educational institutions. Consistorial leaders based their lobbying efforts upon two main conceptual foundations: utility and equal treatment under the law. Separate Jewish schools, they argued, would aid in the more efficient integration of Jewish youth, producing economic and moral benefits for the French nation. At the same time, the emancipation of French Jews in 1791 and the recognition of French Judaism as a state religion in 1808 required that Jews have the same opportunities to educate their children as Christians had.[2] In developing this negotiating strategy, consistorial leaders sought to establish a mutual obligation between French Judaism and the French state that could then translate into financial and political support. For their part, French government officials focused upon the projected returns on their political and capital investments.

These different approaches to the education issue reveal conflicting conceptions of the proper role of Judaism in the integration process. Both government and consistorial officials believed in the general necessity of French Jewish integration. The determination of just what integration meant, however, proved consistently imprecise. As Pierre Birnbaum has recently observed, Jewish emancipation in France seemed to present two basic options for French Jews: assimilation and "voluntary or involuntary communitarization."[3] Yet succumbing to the temptation to interpret these choices as polarized—that Jews chose one to the exclusion of the other—overlooks the possibility that many French Jews stood somewhere between the two strategies.[4] The way that French Jewish leaders employed the concepts of utility and equal treatment indicates a significant mixing of the two options in consistorial thinking. In negotiating the future of French Jewish education, the consistorial leadership sought to reconcile the demands of integration with the desire to preserve French Jewish continuity, albeit in a more modern form.

This article will explore the impact of this conceptual reconciliation on the Consistory's attempt to develop a national system of Jewish education in the first half of the nineteenth century. As the state-designated overseers of Jewish integration, the consistorial leadership needed to address both civic and religious concerns in its educational plans. One central question dominated the dialogue: should Jewish children attend general French schools or separate Jewish ones in order to speed their integration? Contrasting notions of utility and equality subsequently framed much of the educational dialogue between Jewish leaders and the French authorities. The struggle to define these concepts set the tone for debates that shaped government decisions regarding material and political support for Jewish education, and consequently limited the educational options open to the Consistory.

As much as any other issue of the post-emancipation era, education raised fundamental dilemmas for the leaders of French Judaism. Modern education stood at the center of the consistorial plan for promoting the regeneration and integration of French Jewry. According to this vision, Jewish schools and schoolmasters would produce Jewish youths versed in both their religious heritage and the basic academic skills required for citizenship in the developing French state.[5] Jewish primary schools would also prepare their students—who would come mostly from the poorer ranks of French Jewry—to take up "useful" occupations, such as manual trades and artisan crafts that would theoretically enable them to integrate into the French economy.[6]

This focus, however, placed Jewish schools at odds with the educational priorities of the French government. Most significantly, the regenerative mission meant that Jewish instruction targeted a different clientele than the general French public school system. By contrast, the Napoleonic and Restoration regimes directed their educational resources toward the improvement of secondary education for the first third of the nineteenth century.[7] Such an emphasis made sense: the developing government bureaucracy required the creation of a class of mid-level civil servants trained at French *collèges* and *lycées*. While the Restoration government did issue decrees encouraging primary education beginning in February of 1816, it failed to back these directives in the national budget. Consequently, significant growth of the French primary school system did not begin until the 1820s.[8]

Jewish education, by contrast, needed to concentrate upon primary schooling. In the eyes of both Jewish and non-Jewish educators, most Jewish children lacked the knowledge necessary to attend French secondary schools. Jewish pupils therefore needed to learn elementary subjects such as the French language and basic arithmetic in order to participate successfully in French social and economic life. These subjects fell under the domain of primary education. As a result, while the general French system concerned itself with polishing the abilities of more advanced students to serve state needs, consistorial educators worked to create a Jewish student pool equipped with rudimentary scholastic skills.[9] In their initial negotiations with state authorities, consistorial leaders needed to demonstrate the usefulness of Jewish institutions to government officials with an entirely separate educational vision.

Later developments rendered the consistorial agenda equally problematic. The expansion of the French school system, particularly at the elementary level, compelled Jewish educators to explain why acculturation required separate Jewish institutions. From the government's point of view, the growing presence of communal schools negated the need for specifically Jewish institutions. Indeed, to many of these officials French public schools represented the most efficient vehicles for the process. In order to make a utilitarian case for separate Jewish schools, the Consistory needed to demonstrate that their institutions possessed the unique ability to bring the mission of integration and regeneration to fruition.

While consistorial leaders certainly favored an educational system that would facilitate integration, their lobbying tactics reveal that they also perceived limits to the process. Justifying separate schools on the basis of equal treatment under the law meant an assertion of French Jewish legitimacy. In other words, a role for Jewish education in integrating France implied the validity of one's existence as a Jew. Arguments for fair treatment thus acknowledged a separation between the civic sphere of citizenship and the personal sphere of religious self-identification. Utilitarian arguments sought to show that, far from undermining the goals of emancipation, a degree of Jewish distinction would produce benefits for France as a whole. Combining these two ideas enabled consistorial leaders to argue that Jewish continuity remained consistent with, and could even facilitate, both Jewish integration and French national development. The Assembly of Notables and the Great Sanhedrin convened by Napoleon in 1806 had asserted the basic moral compatibility between Judaism and French citizenship. By linking fairness and utility, the Consistory reinforced this compatibility, uniting Judaism with Frenchness while simultaneously preserving and strengthening both. An acculturated Judaism conforming to general social and cultural norms—what Pierre Birnbaum has called "Franco-Judaism"[10]—thus represented a legitimate expression of one's Frenchness.

This view of the role of Judaism in crafting a wider national identity for French Jews finds an interesting parallel in the case of the learned societies popular among middle-class Frenchmen of the nineteenth century. Members of these societies—sometimes called "emulation societies"—saw similar relationships between the civic and personal spheres. The emulation society created a space that united its members, who might come from various occupational, educational or even economic backgrounds, with interests of a higher purpose such as science, knowledge, or self-improvement.[11] For French Jews, a similar view of the civic sphere existed, one in which Frenchness united citizens of all religions for the public good.

The concept of utility became the most powerful idea linking Jewish schooling to this higher purpose. One could most effectively argue the necessity of separate schools by emphasizing their benefits for France. In formulating their positions on this vital issue, consistorial leaders turned to the broader French educational *milieu*. Most frequently, they drew upon the reasoning proffered by advocates of French moral education. According to this school of thought, the formation of loyal and productive citizens depended upon a healthy moral and ethical structure. A sound French education therefore could not entirely ignore those religious teachings that promoted moral advancement.[12] This position represented a middle ground between those who favored complete secularization of education and those disposed toward deepening religious—meaning Catholic—involvement in French schools.[13]

The consistorial leadership applied this thinking to the Jewish situation. Any proper education, they argued, had to attend to the moral formation of its pupils. If religion formed the basis for human morality, Judaism then served the same function for Jews. Jewish children therefore required a healthy dose of Jewish religious instruction in order to become moral and productive citizens. Because consistorial schools served large numbers of poorer Jewish children, the emphasis upon moral development and economic functions assumed added importance.[14] According to moral education advocates, poverty resulted from—and contributed to—a deleterious moral malaise for which religion offered a powerful antidote. By preserving the Jewish religion in an era of rapidly advancing disbelief, Jewish schools would address both the economic and cultural development of French Jewry while simultaneously reinforcing the moral underpinnings of French society. An early consistorial petition therefore stressed the urgency of establishing Jewish schools in order to build a moral foundation for Jewish schoolchildren. Pupils lacking such instruction, they wrote, stood at risk of becoming "immoral men, dangerous to society and to the state."[15]

The Consistory also had to address ongoing discord within French Jewry regarding the function and content of Jewish education. Its program faced opposition on two fronts. One party—led by the writer and vocal advocate of Jewish reform, Olry Terquem[16]—objected to the contradictory goals of integration and separate Jewish education. This group wished to accelerate Jewish integration and echoed governmental concern that separate schooling would only impede Jewish entry into French society.[17] More traditionalist Jewish factions saw the secular components of consistorial education as a danger to Jewish tradition and a pathway to religious indifference. They feared that a school curriculum bifurcated between secular and religious studies would produce students with less knowledge of—and weaker ties to—Jewish tradition. Distrust of the consistorial program encouraged the persistence of traditional *hederim*, especially in the Upper Rhine. These "clandestine" schools in Alsace and Lorraine operated in defiance of both consistorial authority and government decree, but with the approval and support of local populations.[18] This segment of French Jewry would also support the oppositional actions of the Alsatian *grand rabbin* Salomon Klein, who later in the century rejected what he perceived as the integrationist approach of consistorial education and set up his own religious academy outside the rubric of the authorized Jewish administration.[19] Within this volatile context, the Consistory's educational plans needed to balance the state's assimilationist objectives with the poles of educational debate within French Jewry.

Utilitarian arguments also collided with material realities. While government expenditures for education grew steadily through the nineteenth century, the brunt of the financial responsibility for elementary education lay with municipal administrations. In many cases, local authorities lacked the will or the means to support separate confessional schools. As a result, some communes provided more support for primary schools, others less. This uneven situation provided a main impetus for the Guizot school law of 1833.[20] The new law, however, exacerbated these conditions. While it assigned control over school curricula and personnel to the national authorities in Paris,[21] the practical details of primary schooling remained squarely upon the shoulders of the local authorities. The Guizot Law charged the communal councils with organizing primary schools and with providing the bulk of the necessary material resources. Communes also had to supply teachers with lodgings, a salary, and suitable locales in which to conduct their lessons. While the central government continued to subsidize individual local institutions, the Guizot Law delegated wider fiscal responsibilities to communal authorities. As a result, local factors weighed more heavily in the expansion of public education.

Under these conditions, local civil support for Jewish schooling remained inconsistent.[22] In fact, the Guizot Law placed Jewish institutions at an even greater political—and thus material—disadvantage. True, Article 9 of the law allowed for the establishment of more than one confessional public school in a single commune. Civil authorization for such an institution, however, depended upon the consent of municipal officials who would also bear the ensuing fiscal responsibility. By requiring each commune to establish a primary school, the Guizot Law created a rationale for communes either to ignore demands for sectarian education or to favor one religious group over another. The Christian Brothers, for example, reaped particular benefits from communes who opted to turn over their schools to the order. Catholic education also began to make deeper inroads on an institutional basis throughout France.[23]

Jewish school plans therefore had to satisfy several different notions of utility in order to succeed. What the central authorities in Paris deemed useful did not always match the determinations of the municipal or departmental authorities. In a broad sense, "utility" signified the state's approval of an activity or institution as worthwhile and acceptable. The power to make that assessment, however, belonged to the state alone and the definition could vary as the civil authorities saw fit. In the case of Jewish education, state officials tended to consider an institution's contribution to the public welfare and the perceived return on any public money invested in the operation. Municipal officials might add to this list prejudice and local economic conditions, obstacles not necessarily open to broad philosophical argument.

Utility, though, presented even more complexities for the consistorial leadership. Arguing the usefulness of Jewish schooling in the integration process meant at least a tacit acknowledgement that French Jewry had not yet integrated. Petitioning for government aid on the basis of utility meant that consistorial leaders at once pointed toward the incomplete nature of Jewish integration while simultaneously asserting their compliance with the terms and expectations of emancipation. The Consistory's utilitarian arguments thus contained both an admission of its own shortcomings and a criticism of poorer, less cosmopolitan French Jews. While acculturated French Jews could concede this distinction at the beginning of the nineteenth century, it became less palatable for consistorial leaders to admit as the decades passed. Utilitarianism required the efficient use of government funds for the public good; admitting any failures undermined this argument at its very roots.

Ultimately, the state's power to define "utility" framed the educational issue to the Consistory's disadvantage. Jews constituted less than one percent of the French population and could not base their case on sheer numbers. Establishing utility became even more difficult as the government defined the concept according to its own priorities. Consequently, consistorial leaders sought to portray their programs as activities that would help to preserve Judaism while simultaneously promoting the regeneration and integration of French Jews. The state, on the other hand, looked to receive the greatest return on the money it spent while advancing its conception of the public interest. Narrow utilitarian reasoning alone therefore promised little hope for success.

To mitigate these factors, the Consistory introduced an additional line of argument: the concept of fair and equal treatment under the law. This concept appealed to the promises of religious liberty contained within the Declaration of the Rights of Man and Citizen, the French Constitution, and the 1791 decree emancipating French Jewry. Having received emancipation, French Jews should enjoy the same consideration that the government showed to French Catholics and Protestants. By extension, French Judaism should occupy a status equal to Catholicism and Protestantism. Jewish leaders had raised the fairness principle with the Napoleonic regime in their petitions for the formation of the Consistory itself. Not surprisingly, they employed similar arguments in seeking budgetary support for Jewish schools and other consistorial institutions.[24]

The fairness strategy, however, contained its own shortcomings. Most significantly, this line of argument implied a criticism of the state. Calling for fair treatment suggested the *unfairness* of existing circumstances. To accept this argument, the government would have to admit that it had not upheld its side of emancipation. In addition, the fairness strategy raised charges within government circles that Jewish leaders sought preferential treatment for their relatively small numbers of schoolchildren instead of contributing to the common, public French educational system.

The individual pratfalls of both negotiating strategies compelled Jewish leaders to attempt to unite them whenever possible. Appeals for fairness *could* appear as lobbying for special treatment if not properly grounded in utilitarian logic. Similarly, utilitarian reasoning alone made little impact. Jewish schools, which were small in size and in number, often escaped the attention of ministerial officials. Consistorial lobbying therefore had to balance notions of special consideration with fairness on the basis of utility. While the consistorial leaders—who considered themselves fully patriotic Frenchmen—certainly felt a personal attachment to egalitarian ideals, the appeal to fairness also added weight to their utilitarian positions. The utility of Jewish education came to rest in the state's moral interest in meeting its obligations to treat all of its citizens equally, as well as in the unique ability of Jewish schools to advance the cause of integration.

The effort to obtain communal status for the Jewish school in the town of Sarrebourg illustrates the problematic interaction of these factors. In 1842, a group calling itself the Comité communal d'instruction primaire israélite filed a petition appealing for the communalization of the local private Jewish school. Communalization would render the municipality responsible for providing both a suitable locale for the school and a salary for its faculty.[25]

Above all, the Sarrebourg petitioners sought to establish the school's utility and the government's obligation to support it. The school served more than fifty Jewish boys and girls who received instruction in both secular and religious subjects from a certified teacher and his assistant. The religious component of the curriculum, they wrote, played a crucial role in the school's program. The Jewish environment made the school accessible to pupils from traditional families, opening a door to general knowledge for children whose parents would not have permitted them to study with the non-Jewish schoolmaster at the local communal school. Despite the vital service it provided and the void that it filled, the school had received no municipal support. Its only funding came from the students' parents, who paid both the teachers' salaries and the school's material expenses.[26] Certainly, the petitioners concluded, the equal status of French Judaism under the law obligated the commune to support a Jewish equivalent to the instruction provided for Christian children.

Sarrebourg's municipal council, however, disagreed. In rejecting the funding request, its members questioned the logic of maintaining a separate Jewish school when the town already operated a communal school open to children of all religions. The communal school, they argued, provided adequate instruction and took care to respect the beliefs of its Jewish pupils. The presence of twenty Jewish children within the total student body of 160 offered additional proof of the communal school's suitability. Furthermore, the council held that funding a specifically Jewish institution would detract from the education it provided to the children of other religions.[27] Like their non-Jewish counterparts, the Jewish children of Sarrebourg could receive a "complete education" in the public school while exercising "a perfect liberty of belief." Several of the public school's Jewish students had even won academic prizes and had received municipal help in meeting their expenses at the *école supérieure*. Finally, attendance at the communal school could only prove "advantageous" to the Jews in "ending [their] isolation and enabling their children to absorb the mores of French society."[28] The council's understanding of utility thus trumped Jewish claims for fairness. Indeed, for the Sarrebourg council, the fairest course of action was also the most sensible and efficient.

The fairness argument rang hollow elsewhere within the local administration. The Comité Communal d'Instruction Primaire of Sarrebourg, which supervised primary education in the town, also rejected the Jewish petition. It agreed with the municipal council that the existing communal school adequately accommodated children of all religions. The municipal authorities, it noted, had never heard any complaint against the instruction of Jewish children at its school. Equally important, the town lacked the resources to operate an additional primary school.[29]

Concerns regarding the integration process reinforced the committee's ideological objection to separate schooling. The committee argued that if the Jews established their own public school only Jewish children would attend it. A Jewish communal school would therefore create "a point of separation" which the town wished to avoid as it sought to combat the prejudices "that unfortunately subsist even now in this district." The participation of Jewish children in the common educational system with non-Jewish children, by contrast, would redound to the Jews' benefit by accelerating their integration. Moreover, a separate school would not serve the interests of enough of the town's inhabitants to justify the expenses it would generate. Lastly, the committee did not detect any great demand among Sarrebourg's Jews for a specifically Jewish communal school. Despite the existence of the Jewish private school "a great number of families" sent their children to the communal schools, even to the girls' school operated by a Catholic teaching order.[30] While the committee's assessment contained some strikingly convoluted logic—that the failure of the Jews of Sarrebourg to utilize a separate communal school that did not exist obviated the need for such an alternative—its report nevertheless employed utilitarian arguments to refute the petitioners' arguments for equal treatment.

The committee's recommendations met with wide acceptance within the civil administration. The Comité d'Instruction Primaire of the Strasbourg district and the *sous-préfet* of Sarrebourg both agreed that the small number of Jewish school-age children—which they estimated as only about forty boys and girls—hardly justified a separate school. Their attendance at the existing communal schools encouraged contact between children of different religions, created a spirit of "tolerance and union" in the town and thereby advanced the progress both of primary education and Jewish integration.[31] Both the Rector of the Nancy Academy and the Prefect of the Meurthe echoed these opinions and advised the Minister to refuse the request.[32] The Minister concurred and soundly rejected the Sarrebourg petition.[33]

The Sarrebourg episode illustrates the confluence of factors that impeded the Consistory's educational plans. While advocates of separate Jewish schools grounded their arguments upon principles of equality, government officials adhered to more utilitarian standards. In order to receive official sanction—and thereby regular civil financial support—a school had to serve a Jewish population of some size that would otherwise have had to go without primary schooling. Hamstrung by small numbers and insufficient resources, very few Jewish communities could satisfy these criteria.

Local Jewish populations also proved to be insufficient and unreliable sources of financial support for Jewish schools. Ideological opposition to separate Jewish primary schooling emanated from within French Jewry as well as from external sources. One of the most serious objections concerned the credibility of the schools and their teachers among the populations they sought to serve. The aforementioned "clandestine" Jewish schools of the Upper Rhine not only symbolized skepticism regarding modern education; they helped to perpetuate attitudes supporting Jewish religious and cultural conservatism in the region.[34] These institutions offered a more traditional Jewish education, eschewing much of the secular curriculum offered by the communal and consistorial schools. The observation that half of the school-age Jewish children of Sarrebourg availed themselves of the publicly supported primary schools, for example, meant that half of the Jewish children did not. Whether they sent their children to clandestine schools, public schools, or no school at all,[35] half of the Jewish families in Sarrebourg refrained from sending their children to the consistorial school. Their reticence illustrates that neither French nor consistorial schools broadly appealed to Alsatian Jews, many of whom opposed consistorial authority generally.

This absence of enthusiasm meant that even Jewish populations possessing the funds to expand Jewish schooling often lacked the will to do so. Deficient support also threatened the continued maintenance of existing schools. A fundamental problem lay in the economic condition of Jewish populations in the areas targeted by Jewish educators. While the Jews of Alsace did have their grandees, the clientele served by the schools consisted mostly of children whose families occupied the lower end of the economic scale.[36] As a result, the schools had trouble raising money from the people most likely to use their services.

Ironically, the state's assumption of the Jewish religious budget in 1831 created additional financial impediments. While the measure insured the survival of many Jewish religious institutions, it also removed Jewish schools from the jurisdiction of the Ministry of Religions. Consistories could still contribute funds towards Jewish schooling, but the new regulations placed Jewish schools under the administrative supervision of the Ministry of Education. Consequently, the new religious budget provided no regular allocation for Jewish primary education. This change in the system placed existing Jewish schools under increasing financial pressure. Shortly after the law's passage, the president of the Jewish school committee in Nancy observed that his school would suffer enormously from this change. Prior to 1831, the Nancy Jewish school had derived the bulk of its funding directly from the Jewish religious budget.[37] With Jewish schools under the jurisdiction of the Ministry of Education, however, the local authorities had demonstrated less than enthusiastic support for separate Jewish schooling. Institutions such as the Nancy school thus found themselves deprived of a vital financial resource upon which they had come to depend.[38] This situation impelled the Jewish school committee of Nancy to seek aid from the departmental administration, which perfunctorily responded that the school was the fiscal responsibility of the commune. The town of Nancy, though, had allotted only 120f per year, hardly enough to meet the costs of running the school. Despite the subsequent augmentation of this sum to 160f, the school's situation remained precarious. The president finally appealed to the Ministry for aid, warning that the Jewish school might have to close its doors in the absence of governmental financial help.[39]

The establishment of an official Jewish religious budget also diminished the willingness of some Jews to lend financial assistance to the schools. The Marseille Consistory, for example, complained that the government's assumption of the Jewish religious budget had created the impression among its constituents that the state would now provide for all of French Judaism's material needs:

> Our coreligionists who had never before refused the tribute of their zeal and beneficence ... [now believe] that we ought to apply to the Government ... which will not hesitate to lighten their burdens by tossing to Jewish primary education some scraps of the nourishment of which the other schools of the realm partake.[40]

The school committee of the Bordeaux Consistory offered a similar assessment. The Jewish school at St-Esprit, it wrote, served only about twenty students though it could easily have accommodated sixty-five or seventy-five if adequately supported. The new budgetary arrangement, however, made it harder to procure funds. "When the Consistory could levy contributions upon the Jews [*israélites*], an article existed in the local budget of St-Esprit for furnishing the expenses of this school which [in the past] had raised 1500f."[41] The municipal council had extended 300f of aid in 1830 after the Christian Brothers had taken over the communal school, which would thereafter no longer admit Jewish children.[42] Between the municipal allocation and donations from the Jewish community, the Jews of St-Esprit had hired a Jewish schoolteacher. Following the State's assumption of the Jewish religious budget, "voluntary donations promptly exhausted the good will or the faculties of the *israélites* of St-Esprit and Bayonne." The resulting shortage of funds prevented the St-Esprit school from expanding its operations.[43]

Creating a system of modern Jewish education therefore presented a difficult conundrum for consistorial leaders. While they considered education crucial to Jewish integration, Jewish schools seemed to reinforce the very separation they proposed to combat. Jewish educators therefore needed to establish the utility of separation in order to justify the corollary entitlement of Jewish schools to government support. As mentioned previously, they sought to do so using moral arguments: separate Jewish education, in this context, became a narrowly focused means to a wider end. This strategy required the inextricable linking of equality and utility: in order to achieve Jewish integration most efficiently, the French government had to treat Judaism—and in this case, Jewish schooling—equally.

Such reasoning, however, could not completely resolve the apparent contradiction between French and Jewish educational aims. While the state authorized the existence of separate Jewish schools in 1812, it never viewed them as a high priority. As more responsibility for public education fell upon the local authorities, state money for Jewish schooling dried up completely. Jewish schools thereafter depended upon the benevolence of municipal officials and French Jews themselves, both of whom often lacked the means or the will to support these operations. As a result, Jewish schools became largely specialized, philanthropic institutions catering to poor and immigrant Jews. Eventually, the Consistory abandoned its quest for a national system of Jewish primary schools and began to emphasize supplemental programs of religious education.

CONTRAST: THE RABBINICAL SCHOOL

By contrast, consistorial lobbying for a modern rabbinical school more effectively linked conceptions of utility and equal treatment. This success resulted, however, largely from a unique set of circumstances. First, in creating the Consistory in 1808, the Imperial government had charged it with facilitating the mission of integration. While the Consistory's charter legislation did not specifically mandate a reorganization of the French rabbinate, its early leaders saw "modern" French rabbis as agents of modern culture that would result in a transformation of French Jewry. The commission of Jewish lay leaders convened by Minister of Religions Jean-Etienne Portalis in 1805 argued that properly trained French rabbis could at the very least "edify their listeners in the French language."[44] Toward this end, the commission suggested a rabbinical education system designed to train rabbis in both secular and religious subjects. Its final report, the *Plan d'organisation du culte juif en France*, recommended the establishment of two rabbinical seminaries: one in northern France ("Nancy, Strasbourg, or Metz") and one in the Midi ("at Bordeaux or Bayonne"). While the Napoleonic government never implemented this plan, its provisions echoed clearly in subsequent consistorial lobbying.

The consistorial leadership modeled its program along similar lines. French rabbis would learn the French language, adhere to French customs and social conventions, and promote similar behavior among their congregations.[45] While the Consistory's organizing legislation left the exact method of Jewish integration ambiguous, it nevertheless tied the Consistory—and thereby the state of which it was an extension—to the general goal. When the consistorial leadership suggested the creation of a modern rabbinical school, they did so on the basis of this implicit obligation. For their part, French officials within the Ministry of Religions largely accepted the idea in principle, though they haggled over the details for nearly twenty years.

The absence of any equivalent institution in France also lent weight to the utilitarian side of the Consistory's argument. While traditional communities operated their own Talmudic academies, one could not receive modern rabbinical training anywhere else in France. The distinctive quality of modern rabbinical education rested in its systematic combination of secular learning with traditional Jewish subjects.[46] By melding secular and religious instruction, the rabbinical school was intended to create a distinctly French rabbinate that would in turn develop a distinctly French Judaism that would encourage productive Jewish citizenship. Finally, from the state's point of view the rabbinical school would further extend government control over French Judaism. Budgetary arrangements reinforced this mutual understanding of state supremacy. After the institution of the Jewish religious budget in 1831, only officially recognized French rabbis could draw state salaries, even though local communities might accept leaders who had not graduated from the consistorial rabbinical school or received a consistorial stamp of approval.[47] The education of a modern French rabbinate thus fit the general integrationist plans of both ministerial and consistorial officials, though serious differences arose in discussions of curricular details.[48]

Consistorial plans initially envisioned a national, vertically integrated system of Jewish education providing elementary and secondary instruction with a modern rabbinical school as the capstone.[49] Berkovitz and Albert have each observed that this drive to include secular studies as a significant part of rabbinical training originated within the government rather than within the Consistory itself.[50] The provisions outlined in the *Plan d'organisation*, however, clearly demonstrate that this outlook also pervaded the Jewish leadership. Jewish leaders appear to have understood from the beginning the necessity of establishing a utilitarian basis for rabbinical education in order to win government authorization. In so doing, they emphasized the program's benefits both for French Jewry and for France as whole, and the logical implications of the government's stated desire to treat all three religions equally. Fairness and utility therefore intersected for both Jewish and civil officials. While many of these Jewish leaders did seek to create a more modern rabbinate, secular training could only enhance the image of rabbinical education in the eyes of the civil authorities. The government, they realized, would never authorize a Jewish educational program that failed to include a significant secular component. In this sense, the government did act as ideological agent: the Consistory needed to operate within a predetermined set of guidelines in order to gain State support. Consistorial proposals for rabbinical training in the early nineteenth century thus emanated from practical considerations as much as from ideological goals.

In lobbying for state authorization, the Consistory again sought to unite the school's utility with the concept of equal treatment. In the early stages, consistorial leaders stressed the concept of fairness. The state's recognition of Judaism as an official religion, they argued, implicitly authorized French Jewry to educate its clergymen. At the same time, Judaism's equality with other official religions demanded parallel institutions for training Jewish clergy.[51] The Christian religions possessed their own clerical training institutions; the principle of fairness thus dictated authorization of a Jewish rabbinical academy. The first detailed petition submitted to the Napoleonic government also pointed toward the utilitarian necessity of modern rabbinical training for the proper promotion of integration among French Jews. Specifically, the Central Consistory questioned the logic of authorizing a religion and placing certain obligations upon its members while simultaneously restricting it from training clergymen to fulfill those obligations.[52]

As time went on, utilitarian criteria gained greater prominence in the dialogue. This shift resulted from two main forces. First, the fairness argument made little headway with the Imperial administration. In 1812, for example, the Minister of Religions wrote that French Jewry constituted such a small population that one questioned whether establishing Jewish schools of any sort even warranted "the attention of the government."[53] Since numbers alone could not justify a modern rabbinical school, the Consistory needed to establish a stronger rationale. Second, when the restored Bourbon monarchy returned to power in 1816, it found its financial resources considerably limited. Its budget contained a small allocation for education, concentrating mainly upon primary schooling and the French University. Under these circumstances, the government remained reluctant to commit significant funding to a rabbinical school that would serve a small number of students. In 1816, for example, the Commission de l'Instruction publique wrote that instead of establishing a centralized program for Jewish religious study, it would suffice to designate one rabbi in the eastern departments and one in Bordeaux who would teach Hebrew, Bible, and other religious subjects. The commission accepted the view that encouraging secular learning among French rabbis could only speed the progress of enlightenment and integration among French Jews. This knowledge, however, was available through the French school system and did not require a separate institution.[54]

Consistorial officials absorbed this utilitarian view into their subsequent petitions, taking care to emphasize the benefits of modern rabbinical training. In 1822, for example, the Metz Consistory asserted that all *grands rabbins*[55] should possess the *bachélier-ès lettres* degree.[56] Mastery of the French language and other secular subjects would enable them to serve as cultural models for their fellow Jews, and to combat the dangerous "spirit of indifference which would propagate among our coreligionists."[57] The Paris Consistory later predicted that French rabbinical students would "one day become men capable ... of serving as an example, through their piety and their enlightenment to those whom they are called to guide in their religious and moral duties."[58] The Consistory of Marseille also supported the project, envisioning a new generation of French rabbis educated in both religious and "profane" subjects that would both "represent the nation and earn its respect." These modern rabbis would in turn exercise a positive influence upon "the piety" and "political existence" of French Jews, serving as both the symbols and instruments of successful Jewish integration.[59] Such utilitarian language dominated the debates over the rabbinical school.

As in the case of the primary school negotiations, the consistory's utilitarian reasoning contained certain snares. Most seriously, the emphasis on results obligated the Consistory to satisfy state demands regarding rabbinical training. In seeking to establish the usefulness of modern rabbinical education, the Consistory left the details of "modern education" ambiguous. The state's power of authorization endowed it with the ultimate power of definition, which it determined according to its own educational priorities. Agreeing to a satisfactory course of rabbinical studies subsequently became the greatest sticking point blocking the school's establishment. Consistorial officials submitted numerous proposals over the course of nearly twenty years, with state officials repeatedly rejecting them as insufficiently "modern." Even after the school opened in 1829, both Jewish and government officials continued to criticize the rabbinical education program. Dissatisfaction focused primarily upon the inferiority of training in Latin, Greek, and other subjects standard to secular French secondary education and to Christian theological institutions.[60]

The movement toward modern rabbinical education did not, though, emanate solely from the state administration.[61] Incorporating secular learning also held certain advantages for the school's consistorial advocates. An enhanced secular curriculum served the Consistory's integrationist mission while simultaneously bolstering arguments for the school's utility. Later Jewish leaders such as Adolphe Franck—a member of the faculty of the prestigious Collège Française and a consistorial vice-president who also became deeply involved in the rabbinical school project—championed secular learning, both on its general merits and for its benefits for Jewish integration. For their part, school administrators grasped the necessity of conforming to civil guidelines in order to retain the government's political and budgetary support. Rabbis who spoke French, read Homer, and recited Ovid would convince French officials that state money had been well spent. Consequently, modernizing French rabbinical education was an interactive process involving both Jewish and civil considerations. While the idea of secular education for rabbis did not spring entirely from the state, the government's political prerogatives empowered the French authorities to frame the debate according to their own vision.

The civic relationship between Judaism and the French state, however, also opened the door to Jewish arguments for equal treatment. Fairness once again argued a legal principle that reinforced utilitarianism. In one of its early petitions, the Central Consistory argued that by recognizing Judaism as an official religion, the state had implicitly authorized French Jewry to educate its clergymen. French Catholics and Protestants operated their own clerical training institutions; the principle of equal treatment thus dictated civil sanction for a Jewish rabbinical academy in France. The leadership further questioned the logic of authorizing a religion and placing certain obligations upon its members while simultaneously restricting it from training clergymen to fulfill those obligations.[62] Subsequent communications employed similar reasoning.[63]

As in the case of the primary schools, the consistorial leadership hoped to intertwine fairness and utility in order to immunize their request from charges that they sought special treatment out of proportion to the size of their community. For them, the principle of equal treatment under the law obligated the state to help French Jews educate their clergy. While utility placed rabbinical education firmly in the public interest, equal treatment preserved the right to pursue this activity in a distinctively Jewish way. The principle of fairness thus marked the limits of integrationist policies. By invoking fairness, Jewish leaders united the program's benefits with the logical implications of the government's stated desire to treat all three religions equally.

The fairness argument found some sympathetic ears in the government after the fall of the Empire. In 1816, for example, a draft of an administrative report to the Minister of Religions supported the establishment of Jewish primary and rabbinical educational institutions primarily upon the grounds of equal treatment. Existing law, the anonymous author wrote, appeared to favor them by having charged the government with encouraging the entry of Jews into "useful professions." Further, a clear parallel existed between the status of Judaism and Protestantism under French law. The Protestants, like the Catholics, traditionally presented their own candidates for the degree of *docteur en théologie* to the government, which then made the final determination. The analogous position of the two religions suggested that the process for the Protestants should also apply to the Jews.[64] Although it adopted many of these same arguments, the final report ignored the issue of the rabbinical school and recommended authorizing only the Jewish primary schools.[65] Clearly, the principle of fairness alone could not justify government support for such a small institution in tumultuous times.

Nevertheless, the legality of a rabbinical school remained relatively accepted. Final authorization, however, awaited a more detailed establishment of the rabbinical school's utility, and the determination that supporting it represented a desirable expenditure of public funds. The curriculum became the barometer for reaching this judgment, since the government's definition focused chiefly on the results—in this case, the type of rabbis—the school would produce. Subsequent negotiations to iron out these details took twelve years, during which state officials repeatedly rejected consistorial proposals as insufficiently modern. In the spring of 1828, the Central Consistory submitted what would be its final proposal for the rabbinical school. The plan portrayed the school as a useful tool for Jewish integration and moral development. In order to gain admission, rabbinical candidates would have to be French citizens and at least eighteen years of age. They would need to possess certificates of *bonne conduite* from their local consistories, who would also administer tests in Hebrew, biblical exegesis, Mishna and Talmud, French language, history, and geography. The course of studies united secular and religious subjects. The religious section would include Hebrew, Biblical exegesis, Talmud, and works by Maimonides and Joseph Karo. The regulations also specified that the Talmud professor would be responsible for explaining the decisions of the Sanhedrin and demonstrating "the harmony that exists between our religious beliefs and the laws of the State and obedience to the King." In the same spirit, secular study would follow general French guidelines. Rabbinical students would therefore study Latin, logic, French rhetoric, French history, and mathematics. Instructors in the secular subjects would employ only those books approved by the Conseil Royal de l'Instruction publique and currently used by institutions under the supervision of the University.[66] French rabbinical training thus became both a model of the progress of Jewish integration and a means for furthering the process.

The École centrale rabbinique de France received government approval in 1829.[67] Unlike the elementary schools, the rabbinical school fell under the jurisdiction of the Ministry of Religions, as did the Protestant theological schools and the Catholic seminaries. This bureaucratic arrangement brought certain practical benefits, namely an annual allocation from the government. When the government established the Jewish religious budget in 1831, it included a permanent appropriation for the rabbinical school.

By no means, however, did the Treasury shower the French rabbinate with bagfuls of francs. For much of the century, the school's administrators complained of the institution's meager budget and the Ministry's lack of responsiveness to its financial problems. After the school opened in Metz in 1829, it operated under severe financial pressures that directly affected its viability. In its report to the Ministry in March 1847, for example, the school's administrators observed that the school building had fallen into dangerous disrepair and faculty members were badly underpaid. To address these urgent problems, the commission requested an increase in the state's annual subvention of 10,000f.[68] This increase proved an insufficient remedy. Budgetary shortfalls persisted while the school building physically deteriorated to the point that it became uninhabitable. Even after the school moved to Paris in 1859, financial problems continued to worry its administrators.[69]

Nevertheless, the rabbinical school's unique position within French Judaism clearly aided its survival. Despite its financial problems, the annual government allocation enabled the school to regularize its budget. The financial connection also created a more direct channel for lobbying. By extending funding to the school, the state brought it under the civil administrative umbrella and united its condition with the public interest. Civic financial involvement not only increased the degree of state control; in some cases it created a greater sense of civic obligation toward the school's performance. For example, a critique of rabbinical academic standards within the Ministry of Religions argued that paying rabbinical salaries gave the state both the obligation and the right to require "that they are provided with the knowledge necessary to exercise their functions usefully [*utilement*]."[70] This same interpretation of the relationship enabled the Consistory to solicit civic funding for repairs to the school building during the 1850s. While this relationship did not always lead to the satisfaction of consistorial requests, it did provide firmer ground for the school and its supporters in approaching ministerial officials. Civic money, then, solidified the bond between Judaism and state.

This exploration of utility and fairness demonstrates the degree to which the state influenced the structure of Jewish education in nineteenth-century France. The initial consistorial vision had little chance of success from the start. Having established utilitarian criteria that most Jewish primary schools could never hope to meet, the state could reasonably justify withholding financial support. Its generally negative—or at best, ambivalent—attitude toward separate Jewish schooling carried over to upwardly mobile French Jews, many of whom hoped to advance their children's economic and social opportunities by sending them to French schools. Consequently, consistorial schooling became a mostly charitable enterprise serving the poor, even in cities with relatively large Jewish populations. By the Third Republic, the Consistory acknowledged the impracticality of the venture and began to focus its efforts on programs of religious instruction instead of separate educational institutions.[71] The rabbinical school, on the other hand, occupied a specific niche in the French system that provided access to government support and assistance.

If these educational dialogues turned on the concept of utility, they also suggest the practical limits of the concept of equal treatment. While Jewish leaders repeatedly invoked fairness in their educational plans, the evidence suggests that considerations of fairness barely figured in governmental funding decisions. Fairness arguments ironically gained greater importance in government circles during the 1880s, when the state began to restrict religious influence in the public sphere. As the government reduced the scope of activity open to the Catholic Church, it subsequently began to impose the same measures on French Protestantism and Judaism. Equal treatment at that point represented a threat to civic financial support rather than a means of justifying that support.

With anticlerical politicians attacking the very idea of a religious budget, consistorial leaders replaced their appeals for equal treatment with arguments for the uniqueness of the Jewish situation. In 1885, Edmond de Pressensé[72]—a Protestant moderate, opponent of radical anticlericalism and a political ally of the Consistory—rose in the Senate to protest proposed reductions to the Jewish and Protestant budgets.

These cuts, he claimed, would only exasperate the "poverty" already suffered by the Protestant and Jewish seminaries.[73] Lacking the extensive institutional support structure possessed by Catholic seminaries, the non-Catholic institutions likewise lacked their ability to draw upon either institutional funds or monies generated by their religious administrations. Pressensé thus dismissed the argument of equal treatment as an applicable principle. While the Chamber of Deputies had previously suppressed the budgetary credit for student scholarships—"in order to be consistent with its resolution relative to the Catholic seminaries"—it had preserved the funding "necessary for the expenses of the Jewish and Protestant seminaries because these seminaries have nothing."[74] The Chamber itself had therefore recognized the inherent unfairness of the argument of equal treatment. Developments in the rabbinical curriculum demonstrated this same assertion of Jewish uniqueness. As the assertion of utility had resulted in the inclusion of classical studies at the school, the attempt to assert Jewish uniqueness led to an effort to de-emphasize Latin and Greek in the 1880s.[75]

These new negotiating tactics represented a considerable departure from the traditional consistorial rhetoric. Above all, they signaled that the ideal of an integrated French Jewry—homogeneous within and externally indistinguishable from the French nation—had been superseded by more pluralistic attitudes.[76] French Judaism, it turned out, constituted a unique entity whose institutions were *not* in fact equivalent to those of the Christian religions. Yet that uniqueness did not encompass the whole of French Jewish existence. The Consistory continued to educate modern rabbis and shifted its educational priorities as circumstances dictated. Instead of opening new Jewish primary schools, French Jewish leaders sought to establish more extensive supplementary programs of religious instruction for Jewish children. The balance between Frenchness and Judaism within the consistorial framework had not changed: certainly, the Consistory advocated the same good citizenship it always had, as well as the role of Judaism in promoting positive Jewish morality. The method by which the Consistory would have to pursue that balance, though, had changed significantly.

Charting the course of the Jewish educational dialogue with the state thus helps to identify the boundaries of citizenship and state, of the civic and religious spheres of Jewish life in nineteenth-century France. Education represented among the most sacred of undertakings for acculturating French Jews following the Revolution. The developing French school system marked the path to bourgeois respectability, economic improvement and for many, careers in the civil service. The French school system, however, constituted civic space. Efforts to establish a parallel, state-sanctioned and publicly financed Jewish system therefore represented an attempt to stake out a portion of that civic space to address specifically Jewish concerns. Utility arguments, then, represented a justification of French Judaism's claims for that civic space which the concept of equality made accessible.

When viewed in this context, the dialogues between the Consistory and the government take on broader meaning. The concept of equal treatment assumes an acceptance of differences, be they cultural or in this case religious. Utility, at least as employed by French government officials, implied that the state would tolerate those differences so long as they did not conflict with the national interest. Clearly, these criteria changed as readily as the ruling regimes of nineteenth-century France. The Consistory sought to transcend these shifting sands with universal principles that asserted the rights of French Jewish citizens to preserve some element of those differences. Consistorial tactics indicate a fervent belief that Judaism could coexist with French citizenship and that both could flourish. This broader conception of fairness accounts for the persistence of the strategy amid the changes in external conditions. At the beginning of the nineteenth century, fairness meant the right to receive government support on the same level as Catholicism and Protestantism. By the end of the century when Catholicism came under attack, Jewish leaders attempted to distance Judaism from the Christian religions by employing a different idea of fairness: because Judaism lacked the structure of Catholicism and the same internal means of support, it needed continuous civic assistance to survive. *Utilité*, then, asserted Frenchness while *égalité* affirmed the relevance of Jewishness.

The education question reveals a gap dividing the consistorial and the governmental conceptions of the integration process. Instead of interpreting utility through the lens of fairness—that it was most useful to do what was most fair—the state tended to interpret fairness in terms of utility—that it was most fair to do what was most useful. In short, the most worthwhile religious undertakings would advance state goals in the most [cost-] effective manner. Fairness meant applying this same criterion to Catholic, Protestant, and Jewish institutions. By defining utility according to effectiveness, the state relieved itself of any special obligation to help fund Jewish primary schools.

Within this framework, money played a key role that transcended its material importance. Public funding formed a direct link between the recipient and the state. Government money in turn meant civic sanction and inclusion in the official state apparatus. As our brief examination of the rabbinical school suggests, this relationship also brought the recipient under closer government scrutiny and provided a channel for government influence. The funding process thus consecrated the proverbial Jewish ground of rabbinical training as undeniably French. Seeking state sanction and funding for Jewish education thus held significance beyond the school issue: civic authorization meant civic acceptance, not only of the institutions but of the populations they intended to serve. The Consistory would promote the goals of integration and regeneration, but within a specifically Jewish framework.

This conceptual divide helps to explain why the government viewed the rabbinical school more favorably than it did separate Jewish primary schools. The École rabbinique could make a valid claim to a unique segment of the civic space, for it alone could produce a modern rabbinate according to state guidelines. Jewish primary schools, on the other hand, represented an attempt to move a public activity *beyond* the civic sphere to serve the interests of a small population. The Consistory's utilitarian reasoning could never surmount such an obstacle while a viable public alternative existed. To defuse this objection, the Consistory attempted to link fairness and utility; by contrast, the state's position separated the two principles.

The expansion of the French school system during the nineteenth century only intensified this dynamic. The Falloux Law of 1850 placed greater fiscal responsibility for education upon the communes and departments. It also granted increased teaching privileges and supervisory powers to the Catholic clergy. Both provisions impeded any significant institutional expansion of Jewish primary schooling in France. They also severely eroded the civil financial support available for Jewish schools, and effectively ended any hopes for expanding Jewish primary education on a national institutional basis.

TULANE UNIVERSITY

NOTES

The author wishes to thank the Tauber Center for the Study of European Jewry at Brandeis University and the Memorial Foundation for Jewish Culture for supporting this research.

1. For a detailed study of the Consistory, its history and its functions, see Phyllis Cohen Albert, *The Modernization of French Jewry: Consistory and Community in the Nineteenth Century* (Hanover, 1977).

2. After more than two years of debate, the French National Assembly had extended equal political rights to French Jews in 1791. State recognition of French Judaism came under the Napoleonic regime with the establishment of the Consistory. For a summary see Ruth Necheles, "L'emancipation des juifs, 1887–1795. Aspects intellectuals et politiques," in *Les juifs et la Révolution française*, edited by Bernhard Blumenkranz, (Toulouse, 1976), pp. 71–86, and Paula E. Hyman, *The Jews of Modern France* (Berkeley, 1998), pp. 17–35. For a more specific discussion of the issues, see Frances Malino, *The Sephardic Jews of Bordeaux* (Tuscaloosa, 1978), pp. 27–90. On the Consistory and the recogni-

tion of French Judaism, see Albert, *The Modernization of French Jewry*, pp. 56–61.

3. Pierre Birnbaum, *Jewish Destinies: Citizenship, State, and Community in Modern France*, translated by Arthur Goldhammer, (New York, 2000), p. 7.

4. The dichotomy appears most acutely in a number of important pioneering historical studies of nineteenth-century French Jewry. See for example, Michael Marrus, *The Politics of Assimilation* (Oxford, 1971); and Paula Hyman, *From Dreyfus to Vichy: the Remaking of French Jewry* (New York, 1979). Subsequent works have reconsidered the relationship between the two poles in a more non-linear fashion. See Nancy L. Green, *The Pletzl of Paris: Jewish Immigrant Workers in the Belle Époque* (New York, 1986); and Birnbaum, *Jewish Destinies*.

5. Jay Berkovitz, *The Shaping of Jewish Identity in Nineteenth-Century France* (Detroit, 1989), p. 150.

6. Simon Schwarzfuchs, *Du juif à l'israélite: histoire d'une mutation* (Paris, 1989), pp. 263–265; and Paula Hyman, *The Emancipation of the Jews of Alsace* (New Haven, 1991) p. 113.

7. As Robert Anderson has written, the Imperial and Bourbon governments considered "primary schools and primary teachers . . . to be only marginally part of the University, and the policy-making machinery [of the central government] was . . . geared to middle-class education." See his *Education in France, 1840–1870* (Oxford, 1975), pp. 6–7.

8. Joseph N. Moody, *French Education Since Napoleon* (Syracuse, 1978), pp. 20–22; and Raymond Grew and Patrick J. Harrigan, *School, State, and Society: The Growth of Elementary Schooling in Nineteenth-Century France* (Ann Arbor, 1991) p. 47.

9. See Schwarzfuchs, *Du juif à l'israélite*, pp. 268–269.

10. Pierre Birnbaum, *Anti-Semitism in France: A Political History from Léon Blum to the Present*, translated by Miriam Kochan, (Oxford, 1992), pp. 29–82 (originally published as *Un mythe politique: La "République juive,"* [Paris, 1988]).

11. Carol E. Harrison, *The Bourgeois Citizen in Nineteenth-Century France: Gender, Sociability, and the Uses of Emulation* (Oxford, 1999), p. 54.

12. For a brief overview of this school of thought, see Moody, *French Education Since Napoleon*, pp. 18–20.

13. Conflict surrounding the religious content of French public schooling predated the First Empire and continued throughout the nineteenth century. For a summary of the early course of the debate under the Directory and Consulate, see Isser Woloch, *The New Regime: Transformations of the French Civic Order, 1789–1820s* (New York, 1994), pp. 194–199. For the Second Empire, see Anderson, *Education in France*, especially pp. 108–129. For the Third Republic, see Fritz Ringer, *Fields of Knowledge: French Academic Culture in Comparative Perspective* (Cambridge, 1992), pp. 127–140.

14. Hyman, *The Emancipation of the Jews of Alsace*, pp. 109–111.

15. Letter from the Consistoire Central to the Ministre des Cultes, February 7, 1810, F^{19} 11028.

16. For more on Terquem's life and activities, see Jay Berkovitz, *The Shaping of Jewish Identity in Nineteenth-Century France* (Detroit, 1989) pp. 119–126, and 137–138; Richard Menkis, "Les frères Elie, Olry et Lazare Terquem," *Ar-*

chives juives, Vol. 15 (1979): 58-61; and Michael A. Meyer, *Response to Modernity: A History of the Reform Movement in Judaism* (New York, 1988), pp. 165-167.

17. Berkovitz, *The Shaping of Jewish Identity in Nineteenth-Century France*, pp. 152-153.

18. Hyman, *The Emancipation of the Jews of Alsace*, pp. 101-103. In this regard, the Jewish experience mirrored general French tensions. Competition between French private and public schools in general had existed since the Revolution, with the private schools often gaining the advantage. See, for example, Woloch, *The New Regime*, pp. 194-216.

19. See Hyman, *The Emancipation of the Jews of Alsace*, especially pp. 80-85 and p. 102-103; Albert, *The Modernization of French Jewry*, pp. 254-255, 295-296, and 301-302; and Jonathan Helfand, "French Jewry during the Second Republic and Second Empire (1848-1870)," Ph.D. diss., Yeshiva University, 1979, pp. 142-144.

20. Grew and Harrigan, *School, State and Society*, pp. 31-32.

21. A decree of 1834, for example, outlined a class schedule for all French public primary schools. See François Furet and Jacques Ozouf, *Reading and Writing: Literacy in France from Calvin to Jules Ferry* (Cambridge, 1982), p. 137.

22. For an extensive review of the financial issues of Jewish education in France, see Jeffrey Haus, "The Practical Dimensions of Ideology: French Judaism, Jewish Education and State in the Nineteenth Century," Ph.D. diss., Brandeis University, 1997, pp. 140-196.

23. Woloch, *The New Regime*, p. 226; Grew and Harrigan, *School, State and Society*, pp. 91-100.

24. To be sure, this line of argument had predated the Revolution, most notably in the work of the Jewish intellectual Zalkind Hourwitz. See Frances Malino, "The Right to be Equal: Zalkind Hourwitz and the Revolution of 1789," in *From East and West: Jews in a Changing Europe, 1750-1780*, edited by Frances Malino and David Sorkin, (Oxford, 1990), pp. 85-106. See also her *A Jew in the French Revolution: The Life of Zalkind Hourwitz* (Oxford, 1996), especially pp. 29-60.

25. Letter from the Comité communal d'instruction primaire to the Ministre de l'Instruction publique et des Cultes, August 20, 1842, F[17] 12515.

26. Ibid. In fact, this request specifically came to help assure the salaries of the two teachers. The committee asked that the Minister officially declare the Sarrebourg school an "a communal primary school, and that the teachers enjoy the salary fixed by the laws and regulations."

27. *Extrait du régistre des déliberations du conseil Municipal de la ville de Sarrebourg*, November 6, 1842, F[17] 12515.

28. Ibid.

29. *Extrait du régistre des déliberations du comité communal d'instruction primaire de la ville de Sarrebourg*, November 9, 1842, F[17] 12515.

30. Ibid.

31. *Extrait du régistre des déliberations du comité d'instruction primaire de l'arrondissement de Strasbourg*, November 10, 1842, F[17] 12515, AN. Decision of the Auditeur au Conseil d'État, Sous-Préfet de l'Arrondissement de Sarrebourg, November 17, 1842, F[17] 12515.

32. Letter from the Préfet de la Meurthe to the Ministre de l'Instruction publique, November 24, 1842, F^{17} 12515, AN. Letter from the Recteur de l'Académie de Nancy to the Ministre de l'Instruction publique, November 18, 1842, F^{17} 12515.

33. Letter from the Ministre de l'Instruction publique to the Recteur de l'Académie de Nancy and le Préfet de la Meurthe, January 4, 1843, F^{17} 12515.

34. Hyman, *Emancipation of the Jews of Alsace*, p. 74, 101. This trend mirrored the initial difficulty of public schools in effectively penetrating the French countryside. See for example, Woloch, *The New Regime*, p. 195.

35. Primary education did not become compulsory in France until passage of the Law of March 28, 1882. This law also laicized French education and did away with public school fees. See Phyllis Stock-Morton, *Moral Education for a Secular Society: The Development of Morale Laïque in Nineteenth-Century France* (Albany, 1988), pp. 97-102; and Jean-Michel Gaillard, *Jules Ferry* (Paris,1989), pp. 490-498.

36. For more specific statistics on the frequency of Jewish poverty in Alsace, see Hyman, *Emancipation of the Jews of Alsace*, pp. 45-49.

37. Letter from the President of the Comité israélite de Nancy pour l'Instruction primaire to the Ministre de l'Instruction Publique, June 10, 1831, F^{17} 12514.

38. Léon Kahn, "Histoire des écoles consistoriales et communales israélites de Paris, (1809-1883)," *Annuaire de la société des études juives*, vol. 3 (1884), p. 211.

39. Letter from the President of the Comité israélite de Nancy pour l'Instruction primaire to the Ministre de l'Instruction Publique, June 10, 1831, F^{17} 12514.

40. Letter from the Consistoire de Marseille to the Ministre de l'Instruction publique et des Cultes, October 4, 1832, F^{17} 12514.

41. Comité consistorial pour les écoles primaires de Bordeaux, *Rapport au recteur de l'Académie de Bordeaux*, November 23, 1832, F^{17} 12514.

42. Letter from the Maire de la Ville de Saint-Esprit to the Recteur de l'Académie de Pau, August 22, 1830, F^{17} 12514.

43. Comité consistorial pour les écoles primaires de Bordeaux, *Rapport au recteur de l'Académie de Bordeaux*, November 23, 1832, F^{17} 12514.

44. *Plan d'organisation du culte juif en France, présenté à Son Excellence le Ministre des Cultes, Monseigneur Portalis,* F^{19} 11014. Portalis had charged the commission with formulating a proposal for the reorganization of French Jewry with Napoleonic France. The document is undated, but came in reply to Portalis' inquiry of February 4, 1805. Albert dates the document to April or May, 1805. See Albert, *The Modernization of French Jewry*, pp. 56-57. For a discussion of the specific provisions of the *Plan* and the responses to it, see Malino, *A Jew in the French Revolution*, pp. 175-177.

45. Albert, *The Modernization of French Jewry,* pp. 169, and 265-266; and Berkovitz, *The Shaping of Jewish Identity in Nineteenth-Century France*, p. 192-193.

46. This combination formed the essential core of the movement toward modern rabbinical education in Prussia and Hungary as well. See for example, Noah H. Rosenbloom, *Tradition in an Age of Reform: The Religious Philosophy of Samson Raphael Hirsch* (Philadelphia, 1976), pp. 348-368; Robert Liberles,

Religious Conflict in Social Context: The Resurgence of Orthodox Judaism in Frankfurt am Main, 1838–1877 (Westport, 1985), pp. 116–124; David Ellenson, *Rabbi Esriel Hildesheimer and the Creation of a Modern Jewish Orthodoxy* (Tuscaloosa, 1990) pp. 135–165; and Edward Ullendorff, "The Berlin Hochschule für die Wissenschaft des Judentums: Marginalia–Personalities–Reminiscences," in *Jewish Education and Learning*, edited by Glenda Abramson and Tudor Parfitt, (Harwood, 1994), pp.195–202.

47. As Albert points out, consistorial leaders referred to rabbis lacking official certification as *soi-disant rabbins*, or "self-proclaimed rabbis," and denied them state salaries and privileges. See Albert, *The Modernization of French Jewry*, pp. 254–255.

48. For more on these disputes, see my forthcoming article, "How Much Latin Should a Rabbi Know? State Finance and Rabbinical Education in Nineteenth-Century France," *Jewish History*, Vol. 15, no. 1 (Spring, 2001).

49. Letter from the Consistoire Central to the Ministre des Cultes, February 7, 1810, F[19] 11028, AN. These measures also echoed the hierarchical system of the *Plan d'Organization*.

50. Albert, *The Modernization of French Jewry*, p. 244; and Berkovitz, *The Shaping of Jewish Identity in Nineteenth-Century France*, p.195.

51. Letter from the Consistoire Central to le Grand Maître de l'Université Impériale, October 16, 1809, F[19] 11028, AN [microfilm]. In the same letter, the Consistory requested authorization to open a system of Jewish primary schools.

52. Letter from the Consistoire Central to the Ministre des Cultes, September 29, 1811, F[19] 11028.

53. Letter from the Ministre des Cultes to the Consistoire Central, January 4, 1812, F[19] 11028.

54. Letter from the Commission de l'Instruction Publique to the Ministre de l'Intérieur, October 10, 1816, F[19] 11028.

55. The title of *grand rabbin* represents a higher rank of rabbi in the consistorial system. The title signifies greater Jewish learning, and in the case of nineteenth-century France greater secular learning as well. See my article, "How Much Latin Should a Rabbi Know? State Finance and Rabbinical Education in Nineteenth-Century France," *Jewish History*.

56. The *bachélier-ès letters* degree signifies the successful completion of one's secondary education in France, and at that time [and now] was a prerequisite for university studies.

57. Letter from the Consistoire de Metz & la Comité Cantonnal des Écoles to the Ministre de l'Intérieur et des Cultes, February 17, 1822.

58. Letter from the Consistoire de Paris to the Consistoire Central, February 11, 1827, F[19] 11025.

59. Letter from the Consistoire de Marseille to the Consistoire Central, September 3, 1827, F[19] 11025.

60. For more on the issue of rabbinical curriculum, see my forthcoming article, "How Much Latin Should a Rabbi Know? State Finance and Rabbinical Education in Nineteenth-Century France," *Jewish History*.

61. Albert, *The Modernization of French Jewry*, p. 244; and Berkovitz, *The Shaping of Jewish Identity in Nineteenth-Century France*, p. 195.

Jewish Education in Nineteenth-Century France

62. Letter from the Consistoire Central to le Grand Maître de l'Université Impériale, October 16, 1809, F^{19} 11028. In the same letter, the Consistory requested authorization to open a system of Jewish primary schools.

63. See, for example, the letter from the Consistoire Central to the Ministre des Cultes, September 29, 1811, F^{19} 11028.

64. *Projet de Rapport à l'Empereur pour obtenir un Décret qui accorde un faculté de théologie israélite, et des écoles primaires*, F^{19} 11028.

65. Chef de la 2e division, cultes non-catholiques, *Rapport présenté à Son Excellence le Ministre de l'Intérieur*, April 19, 1816, F^{19} 11028.

66. Consistoire Central, Réglement intérieur de l'École centrale israélite de théologie, May 8, 1828, F^{19} 11025.

67. Jules Bauer, *L'École rabbinique de France, 1830-1930* (Paris, 1930), p. 26. Gaining authorization for a rabbinical school required long, arduous years of lobbying and persistence. Space does not permit a full description of the consistorial effort, which lasted through the fall of the Empire in 1815 and on into the late years of the Restoration. For a more detailed description, see Haus, "The Practical Dimensions of Ideology," pp. 17-62.

68. Commission administrative de l'École centrale rabbinique de France, *Rapport sur la situation de l'École centrale rabbinique de France pour l'année 1846*, March 7, 1847, F^{19} 11025.

69. The rabbinical school moved from Metz to Paris following a protracted attempt to improve its building during the 1850s. For the details, see Haus, "The Practical Dimensions of Ideology," pp. 93-139.

70. *Note*, Ministère de la Justice et de la Culte, author unknown, June 30, 1841, F^{19} 11025.

71. See Haus, "Practical Dimensions of Ideology," chapters 4-6, and 9.

72. Edmond de Pressensé [1821-94] was a religious scholar and historian as well as a politician. He clearly spelled out his moderate views on anticlerical issues in the preface to an intellectual history that he published in 1882: "Through my whole public career I have steadily advocated the complete enfranchisement of conscience, and for this I shall ever plead ... I shall be truly happy if this book ... do[es] something to dispel the fatal misconception that science and conscience, liberty and religion, are incompatible. Such an error may be fatal to the life of a country and a people." *A Study of Origins; or the Problems of Knowledge, of Being, and of Duty* (New York, 1884), pp. xii-xiii.

73. Upon moving to Paris in 1859, the École centrale rabbinique had changed its name to the Séminaire israélite de France. The change occurred largely as an attempt to place the school on an equal footing with its Christian counterparts, and to separate it from its often controversial history in Metz.

74. Ben Mosché, "Culte: le budget du culte israélite au Sénat," *Archives israélites*, Vol. 46, no. 10 (March 5, 1885), pp. 75-76.

75. See, for example, the letter from the Consistoire Central to the Ministre de l'Intérieur et des Cultes, January 12, 1880, F^{19} 11027. For a more detailed discussion of the curricular adjustments, see Haus, "How Much Latin Should a Rabbi Know?" *Jewish History*.

76. Pierre Birnbaum has made a similar argument based upon Jewish responses to anti-Semitic agitation during the Third Republic. See his *Jewish Destinies*, especially pp. 214-251.

Stanley Nash

AUTHORS AND WOMEN AS ANTIHEROES IN AHARON MEGGED'S LATER WORKS

In his latest novel, *Persephone Zokheret*,[1] Aharon Megged returns to his much traveled road of the authorial spoof, or the placing of the writer at the center of a parodic novel in which an author, artist, or intellectual is a principal antiheroic character. An antihero, generally speaking, is an unconventional or unexpected central protagonist who displays prominent weaknesses or flaws. Regarding Megged's works, the term antihero can be defined in one of two ways: First of all, he is "the small man," such as the author Jonas in *Ha-Hai 'al ha-Met* (1965),[2] who lives in the shadow of a great heroic figure. Jonas is dwarfed, haunted, and ultimately consumed by his obsession with a legendary Zionist hero, Davidov. Another example of the subsidiary literary personality is Evyatar Levitin, a selflessly loyal, but envious and resentful literary editor for an acclaimed author, Yosef Richter, in *Mahberot Evyatar* (1973).[3] And yet another "small man" is the sabra historian, Arbel, in *Foigelman* (1987),[4] who sets out to salvage Yiddish culture, as it were, by having the work of the Yiddish poet, Shmuel Foigelman, translated into Hebrew.

Most recently, in *Persephone Zokheret*, the daughter, Avivit, is a rather ordinary schoolteacher who lives in the shadow of her distinguished mother, the poet Gavriella Gat. Mother Gavriella unwittingly torments and exasperates her daughter in an oblique evocation of the mother-daughter dynamic of the Greek myth of the Earth Mother Goddess, Demeter, and her daughter, Persephone, the goddess of the springtime.[5] Mother Gavriella, in turn, experiences what she perceives as ungenerous, unfair, demanding, and "tyrannical" recriminations from her daughter.[6] Additional markers of the daughter Avivit as a literary antihero of the "small man" type are her longings to be a creative writer like her mother, to be loved and accepted by her mother, and also her identification with diminutive heroes in literature, such as those of Y. L. Peretz and Flaubert's "A Simple Soul."[7]

The latter short story is the subject of one important chapter in Victor Brombert's acclaimed study *In Praise of Antiheroes*.[8] Brombert's work has served as an inspiration and a direction finder for me in this paper, as indeed have Megged's own intermittent provocative definitions of the antihero, most particularly in his excellent article of 1966, "Six Characters in Search of a Way Out."[9] I should hasten to point out that I will *not* be dealing here directly with the "schlemiel"[10] subcategory of the antihero, for all the importance of this at least partially comic, or Chaplinesque, type in the early Megged of *Ḥedvah va-Ani* (1953) and *Miqreh ha-Kesil* (1959); then subsequently, with less humor, in *'Asa'el* (1978)[11]; and finally, in *Ga'agu'im le-Olga* (1994).[12] In the latter novel, the highly eccentric and unremarkable protagonist, Albert Giron, is indeed a would-be writer, and at the same time, by his own definition (because he is a faceless, computer-using, clerk) he is a "*shumish*," a nonperson,[13] a border-line schlemiel. Except for some general remarks in our "Afterword and Overview," we will leave this subcategory for another paper; as background, however, the "schlemiel" should be kept in mind.

Secondly, in addition to the "small man," the diminutive and undistinguished literary bystander, a second important paradigm of the antihero for the student of Megged is the great hero himself or herself, who is revealed to have feet of clay. Most frequently in Megged's literary universe, an author serves as this great figure, the one who turns out to be a negative hero, and who challenges our assumptions of perfection. By virtue of this very imperfection in greatness, however, these protagonists express the tragedy of the human condition; imperfection renders the negative hero believable, and, at least occasionally, deserving of our sympathy. Megged has asserted on many occasions that even the most gifted literary artists—let alone the altogether suspect famous professors and literary critics—are not necessarily more decent or moral than the average person. In fact, these famous artists are often ethically deficient. Megged cites the paradox that humanistic authors, such as Gogol and Dostoevsky, held reactionary views. He is surprised that politicians in Israel seek the opinions of authors, and cites many negative characteristics of authors and artists as a group.[14] One of Megged's characters, the famous Ḥedvah from *Ḥedvah va-Ani*, reappears in a later Megged novel, *Ha-Gamal ha-Me'ofef ve-Dabbeshet ha-Zahav* (1982). In that novel Ḥedvah laments the cynicism of writers and asks the narrator, "Is there a connection between literature and ethics?"[15]

Gavriella Gat in *Persephone Zokheret* is a complex figure, who is deracinated, alienated, and painfully removed from the human closeness she craves by virtue of her artistic gift. Her ability with words has separated her from her peers and, presumably, from her daughter as well. Gavriella is a bohemian type who longs to be "like Liv Ullman"—intellectual yet sensuous—but she fears she is not succeeding.[16] Her daughter, Avivit, is the very opposite of her mother. She is prim, proper, and practical-minded, a diligent teacher committed to her students and to

Jewish culture. Gavriella fears for Avivit because of her daughter's overly regimented existence, epitomized by her neat "poodle" haircut. Gavriella writes: "I am sorry for her that she has locked herself up between the kitchen and the children's beds, between the blackboard and her date-book, while her soul is squeezed in the narrow space between the walls without the ability to sprout wings and soar." Gavriella wonders if Avivit's "upstanding and didactic style of dress ... comes to protest against [her mother's] bohemianism...."[17]

A rather surprising premise of the novel is that Gavriella's artistic, bohemian, and ideological predilections are a function of her Greek or Hellenistic leanings. Although her poetry is imbedded with citations from classical Jewish literature and even kabbalah, these appear to be mere ornamental conceits for an artist who is immersed in Greek culture. Her daughter, Avivit, speculates that her own involvement in promoting Judaic consciousness in her teaching and in defending the Hebrew language against foreign expressions must have arisen as a reaction to her mother's "Hellenizing" tendencies.[18] Just one example of Avivit's hypersensitivity on these matters are her thoughts when her children play with the little statuettes in Gavriella's abandoned apartment. She wonders: "What would Mattathias the Hasmonean say about this?"[19] Shades of S. D. Luzzatto![20] Gavriella herself, after her conversion to Orthodoxy, laments: *"yevanim niqbetsu alai ve-timme'u et hekhalai"* ("Greeks ganged up against me and defiled my holy places").[21] In this pun on the lyric of the well-known Hanukkah song, Gavriella laments her erstwhile attraction to Greek aesthetics. Ideologically, too, her Hellenism seems to have led Gavriella to participate in organizations for Mediterranean culture, to a short affair with a musician from Tangiers and to her expression of sympathy for a Palestinian suicide bomber, that so infuriates her husband that this leads to their divorce. All of this background unfolds only as the book advances. The reader is greeted abruptly in the opening pages with what really is the denouement of all of these tendencies: Gavriella has become a *ba'alat teshuvah*, and has married an Orthodox jeweler in the Tsefat Hasidic community.

THE INFLUENCE OF MODELS FROM WORLD LITERATURE

Israeli literature probably has no author more attentive to models from world literature than Megged. Surely, no other Israeli author has so scoured the field in assimilating models of the antihero from world literature.[22] Since the society of writers and artists is the human arena that Megged knows best, he has been a virtuoso in targeting the foibles and limitations of the literary world's cast of characters. But one may also consider Megged in the broader category of the intellectual as antihero. In the course of considering this topic I arrived at two representative models (among many) from world literature: Italo Svevo and Max Frisch. These two writers can be helpful in assessing Megged's strategies. Not that Megged uses the same methods, nor does he quite reach the extraordinarily high level of these writers. Both Svevo, the Italian Jewish author of the 1923 masterpiece *Confessions of Zeno*, and Frisch, the Swiss Jewish author of the novel *Homo Faber*, are the subject of chapters in Brombert's *In Praise of Antiheroes*[23] and they are also cited by Megged.[24] Albert Camus is yet another paradigm of an author who depicts intellectuals as antiheroes. I will not deal with Camus here except to note that one critic already pointed out that a short story by Camus has a very similar premise to that of *Ha-Ḥai 'al ha-Met*, namely an author who is unable to fulfill his contract to write a book.[25]

Megged's characters approximate some of Svevo's self-deprecating ironies and his reflections on life as illness or aberration. The most well-known theme of Zeno's confessions is his lampooning of the fad of psychoanalysis in the context of his efforts to give up smoking and to give up cheating on his wife. In each case Zeno preemptively finds strategies to cling to his putative weaknesses or illnesses, and ultimately this small or weak or maladjusted individual survives and triumphs while the stronger, more "normal," types are destroyed by the collapse of the stock market and political upheavals. Megged hails Svevo's vision of the small man's triumph.[26] However, a difference should be noted: To the degree that Zeno triumphs, albeit clumsily, by his wits, Zeno resembles the picaresque hero, not so much in his being a rogue, but in his achieving success. Contrariwise, Megged's heroes of the "small man" variety usually end up in an unresolved or grotesque—not at all triumphant—state of flight. This follows, as we shall see, Megged's view of the prophet Jonah as the paradigmatic "small man" of world literature.[27]

Megged, as noted, has been absorbed in observing literary models from European and American culture. The author Meyer Levin, while stating in the headline of his review of Megged's *Fortunes of a Fool* (1962) in English translation that the "New Book by Israeli Aharon Megged Could Hold Its Own in Any Language,"[28] criticized Megged for eyeing and trying to imitate the literary techniques of other authors. While Megged abandoned the literary experimentation in his novels of the early sixties, he never stopped comparing his literary goals to that of great masters in other literatures. His literary spoofs and *romans a clef* constantly embrace models from outside of Hebrew literature—as well as models from Hebrew literature. His parodic treatments of protagonists such as Elisheva Tal-Blumenfeld in *Ha-Ḥayyim ha-Qeṣarim* (1972)—a figure reincarnated in *Ha-Gamal ha-Me'ofef ve-Dabbeshet ha-Zahav*—and of course, in that same tour-de-force, of the formidable literary critic Shatz, a kind of hybrid amalgam of Baruch Kurzweil and Dan Miron, all contain considerable information and theoretical models from comparative literature.[29] Our goal then is to shed light on Megged's *oeuvre* not through reducing him to the sum of his real-life models or influences but by enhancing our appreciation for his creative syntheses of these many influences.

YOM HA-OR SHEL 'ANAT AS A PRECURSOR TO PERSEPHONE ZOKHERET

There is some analogy to Max Frisch's weighty reflections on the limitations of *Homo Faber* (literally "man who makes things"—the limitations of materialistic science and values—not only in *Persephone Zokheret* but even more so in Megged's earlier novel of 1992, *Yom ha-Or shel 'Anat*.[30] This earlier novel has received relatively little critical attention, and we will therefore study it here as a parallel and preamble to *Persephone Zokheret*. It may also be noted that both of these novels—as well as Megged's *Duda'im min ha-Aretz ha-Qedoshah* (1998)[31]—have female protagonists as principal characters and that is one of the several features that merit commentary. It is not surprising that Megged views femininity and passivity as traits conducive to the antiheroic posture. In speaking of his antihero paradigm, Jonah, Megged writes: "he is a passive hero, a non-hero. The very name Jonah is 'feminine,' 'weak'...."[32] As I noted in my study of *Duda'im min ha-Aretz ha-Qedoshah* in these pages, Megged's empathy for his hero, a Christian woman artist with lesbian leanings, is a benchmark in his identification with the outsider as antihero.[33]

In *Yom ha-Or shel 'Anat*, the protagonist Orly Altschuler is a budding writer who has had the traumatic experience of deciding to walk out on her fiancé immediately following their wedding night. Orly has been attending a creative writing seminar with an overbearing instructor, Tirtsa Baharav. Orly ultimately walks out on this instructor, too, because the latter, a minor ("small man") literary personality, shares in the quality of pretentious bombast that Orly so abhors. Orly has an eccentric brother, Mishael, a genius who draws analogies between the world of quantum physics and the psychological domain of literature. Mishael is also absorbed with the quasi-mystical implications of configurations and "mathematical" values in the letters of the Hebrew alphabet. Mishael's tangential musings combine with Orly's rejection of Israeli culture in containing a societal critique analogous to that of Max Frisch. Megged's novel depicts an Israeli society that has become so consumer-oriented and commercially driven, that it is spawning new reincarnations of the stereotypical "Jewish merchant."[34]

Reflecting back on the day of her wedding party, Orly writes that she felt like an outsider while the kibbutz members sat around singing obsolete songs of pioneering Eretz Yisrael. For Megged the kibbutz ethos is far more moribund in the 1990s than it was in the 1950s when Shlomik in *Ḥedvah va-Ani* had just left his and Ḥedvah's kibbutz. Hearing an urban *kumsitz* singing "Be-'Arvot ha-Negev" makes Shlomik feel deep pangs of recrimination over abandoning a kibbutz idea that was still quite viable at that time. Not so in the 1990s when profiteering has encroached on kibbutz values and the whole Israeli ethos is apparently questionable in Megged's view, as reflected through the prism of Orly Altschuler. Feeling "left out" at her wedding party, Orly says most ironically, that she is sure that "she will never be the hero of an Israeli novel,"[35] because she can not identify with "*yisre'eliyyut*." (Orly did not say that she would never be the *antihero* of an Israeli novel.) As Orly listens to two self-assured women speaking with "that confidence that is so energetic and boldly opinionated," she thinks to herself, "This is what gives '*yisre'eliyyut*' its character and distinctiveness, this (together with such dubious 'rituals' as the obsessive dicing of vegetables for salad) is what makes [*yisre'eliyyut*] what it is."[36] Orly, therefore, feels pushed aside and unable to participate. And this, in all probability, is what leads Orly to abandon her new, very-much-the sterotypical sabra husband the very first morning after their wedding. Presumably, Orly can not identify with the excitement of her young kibbutz member husband, who now wants to sell enema appliances (*choqanim*) to the Chinese army.[37]

There is something reminiscent of *Yom ha-Or shel 'Anat*'s bashing of Israeli consumerism in *Persephone Zokheret*, although the cultural critique is less prominent in this more recent novel. For all of Avivit's initial horror at her mother's reinventing herself as an Orthodox woman, Avivit returns from Tsefat, after visiting Gavriella and her Hasid husband, wistful about the idyllic life she has witnessed and sadly resigned to rejoining the land of the "malls and materialism, of rock music and emptiness" or, in the more felicitous Hebrew phrase, "*eretz ha-qanyonim ve-ha-qinyanim, ve-haroq ve-ha-riq*."[38] The central thrust of *Persephone Zokheret*, however, is not the moral bankruptcy of Israeli secular society (as it indeed was in *Yom ha-Or shel 'Anat*),[39] but rather the portraiture of the literary antiheroes involved—from Gavriella Gat to her daughter Avivit to the neurotic copy editor.[40]

In both of the novels, *Yom ha-Or shel 'Anat* and *Persephone Zokheret*, we see the kind of merging of the ideological and the literary that Max Frisch excelled in. Especially in *Yom ha-Or shel 'Anat*, Megged casts his material in a more parodic, if not carnivalesque, tone that, as we know from Bakhtin, can often be overtly iconoclastic.[41] The famous fictional author, Meshullam Yariv, author of the novel within a novel, entitled

"*Yom ha-Or shel 'Anat*," receives an invitation to the wedding from Orly's mother. She invites him only out of mere status-seeking and as window dressing. Yariv, for his part, has had a megalomaniacal dream: the twenty-two letters of the Hebrew alphabet, all of them the height of a person, are standing around him in a circle; all but two of the letters, the *alef* and the *lamed*, are bowing down before him. The *alef* and the *lamed* prefigure for this author's grandiose ego the invitation he has received to the wedding of **O**r**L**y **A**ltschu**L**er. He thus feels he should attend this wedding, in spite of the fact that he does not know any of the participants. Continuing with this caricature, Megged tells us Yariv thinks that at the wedding he might also get some material for a popular book about love—a kind of "do-it-yourself" manual—borderline pornography that he considers publishing under an assumed name in order to supplement his income, thus enabling himself to spend more time writing serious literature.[42]

Equally scathing is Megged's portraiture of Orly's creative writing instructor, Tirtsa Baharav, with whom Orly has had a falling-out. Orly clearly tires of this instructor's controlling temperament and her opinionated strictures, such as her directive that the aspiring writer must avoid "the sincerity trap" and keep an "ironic distance." Orly tires of Baharav's overbearing attitude and of her platitudes: "writing is a sickness," writing is a lifelong dedication akin to Jeremiah's calling. Best of all in terms of subtle satire is the instructor's indignant letter after Orly withdraws from Baharav's seminar and hangs up the phone on her instructor. The letter is a brilliant parody of this ego-bruised instructor's retaliation against Orly on the pettiest level.[43]

PERSEPHONE ZOKHERET

Persephone Zokheret contains not only a highly interesting portraiture of the chaotic and misunderstood creative poet, Gavriella Gat, but equally incisive depictions of other individuals on the periphery of the true artist, Gavriella's embittered daughter, Avivit Feingold, and the unnamed literary editor, who pens the following self-indictment (an expanded portrait of the jealousy that Evyatar Levitin in *Maḥberot Evyatar* harbors toward the artistic genius of Yosef Richter):

> All these years that I've been correcting errors of grammar and syntax, inserting commas and periods like scattershot, penciling in and erasing, weeding out errant words and overhauling entire sentences—I feel like someone who gazes at the promised land from afar but will never reach it. Or to use a rather vulgar analogy—like someone who looks on from the side at heated love-making, and he—bumbling idiot that he is—has the audacity to whisper to the lovers how they might improve their performances.[44]

On the human level, the mother-daughter relationship in *Persephone Zokheret* has considerable interest quite apart from literary or intellectual satire, although these dimensions add to the book's fascination. Avivit feels terribly neglected by her mother, whom she regards as a monstrous narcissist. Avivit thinks her mother "did not want her to be born"—that she resents Avivit for "having stolen her freedom from her."[45] The very name Gavriella chose for her daughter—Avivit—was but a symbol for her slain lover, Aviv. Avivit's brother, Nuni, a scientist studying abroad, pleads with, cajoles, and scolds Avivit for being too intolerant of their mother. But Avivit's acute sibling jealousy brings her to misread Gavriella/Nogah's account of her visit with Nuni at his army base as "incestuous."[46] The account is written in a dense stream-of-consciousness form, whereby Megged very cleverly sets up a situation of jealousy-ridden misinterpretation by the insecure Avivit. Gavriella speaks of a love tryst, but this is with her lover, Aviv, and not with her son, Nuni.[47]

Nuni responds angrily to Avivit's inveterate complaining about Gavriella. He maintains that Avivit fails to bear in mind that their mother is an artist, and, as such, she functions on a different level than the average person. He reminds Avivit of Gavriella's hypersensitivity about her art, about an occasion when she was not chosen, passed over, in the selection of a woman poet to represent Israel, and how she suffered intense stomach pains as a result of this.[48] Avivit is aware that she is obsessed—indeed Avivit herself knows that she is too harsh, and that if she were to be judged she could be liable as a *"ben sorer u-moreh,"*[49] the biblical disobedient and reckless child, who is put to death. For her part, Gavriella intermittently thinks of Avivit/"Dina," her daughter, as a "tyrannical saint,"[50] and she, too, characterizes their tense relationship with the gravity of biblical allusions. Her daughter would condemn her, like the biblical *sotah*, to the trial by ordeal of drinking "the bitter waters."[51]

Nuni writes that if their mother were guilty of all the charges Avivit has leveled, that Gavriella would be deserving of Hell. In his most extreme rebuke to Avivit, Nuni makes a comment that draws on the novel's recurrent allusiveness to Greek themes. He accuses Avivit of "matricide," of a reverse Oedipus complex,[52] and thereby evokes and utilizes premodern tropes in reducing modern figures to their most elemental and classically tragic proportions.

THE GREEK ALLUSIONS IN *PERSEPHONE ZOKHERET*

As Brombert demonstrates, for Max Frisch in *Homo Faber* the allusions to Greek mythology are integral to the plot of Frisch's novel and highlight its tragic ironies. Frisch's novel incorporates the telltale theme of the unwitting commission of incest by the hero Walter Faber. This is followed by the death of his daughter (reminiscent of Agamemnon's sacrifice of Iphigeneia), and then Faber's fear that the girl's mother, his onetime girlfriend, will follow the Greek myth and go so far as to kill him in the bathtub, out of revenge. The title *Homo Faber,* as already noted, signifies practical or utilitarian man, "man who makes things," as opposed to *"Homo Sapiens,"* "man who knows," or *"Homo Ludens,"* "man who plays, dreams, and produces in an artistically creative mode." According to Brombert, Frisch gave "play" a central role in life.[53] It is also significant that Megged, too, praises the notion of *Homo Ludens,* man who plays, the title of Erasmus's famous treatise.[54] We need only recall the title of Megged's early major work *Miqreh ha-Kesil (Fortunes of a Fool)* to see the force of Megged's reaction against his onetime commitment to the humorless tenets of Marxism in life and art.[55] Equally, one may view these later works against the backdrop of Megged's earlier dystopia of the 1960s, *Massʻa el Eretz Gomer.*[56] One can see much of Megged's parodic playfulness as a reaction against the stifling seriousness of the Communists' socialist realism that (before 1952) had dominated Israeli artists and writers. And it is more than a coincidence that the historian Arbel diagnoses his own "tragic flaw" as his inability to appreciate poetry or even to concern himself in his work with the human dimension, in the way the great authors of historical novels do. In his self-recrimination after Nora's suicide, Arbel asks himself: "Did I—who during all my years scrutinized facts in finest detail— did I hear the cry of Nora's innermost soul *(Ha'im shamʻati et tsivḥat tsippor nafshah shel Nora)?*"[57]

Much more powerfully than Megged's Arbel, Frisch's Walter Faber laments the tragic outcome of his life. The ironic resonances with Greek myth in Frisch's *Homo Faber* contribute to rendering Frisch's protagonist an immensely poignant antihero, a most effective modernized version of the classic tragic hero. Presumably, it is Walter Faber's inordinate scientific practicality that brings about his downfall. Brombert analyzes Walter Faber's onetime lover, the dead girl's mother, as a figure in this modern Greek drama as well. She is a professor of classical archaeology, and Brombert diagnoses her sin, her "hubris," as that of presuming to be a solitary parent. She has kept secret the fact that Faber was the father of her daughter, so that she would have total possession of the girl. Such is Brombert's reading. The resonances with Greek themes may be imprecise but they are no less real and most artistically inspired.

In *Persephone Zokheret,* along with his numerous allusions to Greek mythology, Megged is also experimenting with allusions to pagan tragedy; to the challenge to Zionism of so-called "Mediterranean" or "Canaanite" sympathies; and generally, to the warring trends in Jewish historiosophy between reaching outward toward universalism and the more exclusivist—some might say, parochial—tendencies of an S. D. Luzzatto, or even an Ahad Ha'am. Each chapter of Gavriella's fictionalized autobiography, "*Pirqe Nogah,*" is preceded by an epigram from classical Greek literature. The friction and resentments between Gavriella and her daughter Avivit are so intense that Gavriella muses: "One day, I fear, an Oresteian tragedy will take place in our family."[58] Gavriella Gat's daughter is named Avivit, and this name attempts to capture or parody the personality of the mythological Persephone, the mournful goddess of the springtime. This is "the legend of the Greek earth goddess Demeter, worshiped as a mother goddess, and her daughter Persephone . . . the maiden who was abducted and made queen of the Underworld by the god Hades, while Demeter, in maternal grief and wrath, made the earth barren."[59] Edith Hamilton in her marvelous account of Demeter and Persephone emphasizes the uniquely human and sorrowful nature of these two goddesses, the goddess of mother earth and the goddess of the springtime.[60] The "human" qualities of these two mythological women clearly endeared them to Megged.

The title of the novel, *Persephone Zokheret*, has only an oblique relationship to the plot of the story. This resembles the indirect allusiveness of the titles in the novels *Ha-Gamal ha-Me'ofef* . . . and *Yom ha-Or shel 'Anat*.[61] In these novels, too, there is only a hint that the title chosen for Megged's novel casts some light on its plot or characters. If we may venture to speculate: the title *Persephone Zokheret* imperfectly recalls the syndrome of an intense conflict-ridden mother-daughter relationship, in which both partners feel grievously wronged and misunderstood by the other. The plot opens with Avivit's recounting of the events leading up to her mother, Gavriella Gat, abandoning her former way of life and marrying into the Tsefat ḥaredi community. Avivit provides the aforementioned literary editor with her own memoirs and letters, as well as the fictionalized biography that her mother had asked her to read as a kind of soul-baring confessional.

THE ANTIHERO'S FLIGHT AND VULNERABILITY

Megged has sketched the notion of a "Pygmalion Syndrome" in the authorial process.[62] There is, he says, a dynamic relationship between an author and his work. In the course of writing an author can "fall in love" with his character and finds that his attitude toward this character has changed. It is our hypothesis that Megged starts out disliking the mother and poet, Gavriella/Nogah, but in the course of the creative process of writing the novel he begins to sympathize with her. The reader's first impression is very negative, learning about Gavriella as he does from the biased perspective of her resentful daughter. By the end of the novel, however, Gavriella appears very much to fit the pattern of Megged's antihero protagonists who end up in a kind of grotesque flight, and merit our sympathy. Megged assesses this flight syndrome in a variety of fictional figures beginning with the prophet Jonah—for him the archetype of the awkward "small man" who "opts out" of life in various ways. This feature of Jonah's "virtuosity" in flight is appealing also, coincidentally, for the poet Zelda.[63]

Gavriella's "flight," too, is certainly grotesque and, like the flight of Jonah, it ends with a question mark, or in the unresolved state of "*tequ*," as Megged describes the flight of many antiheroes, because as Gavriella's former husband states, it is not at all certain that this will be her "last station stop."[64] In the intensity of her search for love and closeness, Gavriella adopts different strategies of withdrawal, and her religious conversion may be just one more permutation of the flight syndrome. By contrast, in Yehoshua's *Ha-Me'ahev* the metamorphosis of the lover into a *haredi* Jew is a totally passive form of flight aimed at caricaturing the insularity and obliviousness of this *haredi* element to Israel's most devastating war. It does not at all resemble the active form of flight of Megged's antiheroes, a flight that makes a statement. Even the son who disappears in *Mass'a be-Av* is rebelling against an ethos of war and militarism in a much more philosophically engaged manner than Yehoshu'a's picaresque hero.[65]

Gavriella Gat's flight in our novel is threefold: first, she flees her own personal hell of paralysis and isolation imposed on her by her gift of words, by her privileged but painful status of being a poet; second, she flees the pain and humiliation of rejection and jealousy—most of which she brings upon herself—in her search for love, affection, and sex (at several junctures, in fact, she expresses disgust with sex[66] on her way to what her daughter calls her "conversion" or "epiphany" and her son calls her "*hitharedut*"[67]); third, she flees, at least symbolically for her daughter, the world of Israeli consumerism, narcissism and value-deficient Israeli secular culture. We will make just a brief point about the latter, the critique of Israeli secular society—since that is not the primary thrust of this novel—and then return to the other points, the lonely plight of the artist and her frustrations in love.

In true Megged style, he describes the bizarre transformation of Gavriella into a demonstrative Orthodox woman who chants out loud in a mock cantorial style, and in company, the words of the liturgy "*ani-ani-ani-ani-ani-ani 'aniti me'od*"[68]—the word '*aniti* being written with an 'ayin. Megged then parodies this with a subtle switch from the word '*aniti*' written with an '*ayin*, meaning "I have become most poor," to the fanciful parodic construction imagined by Avivit as she returns to secular Israel: *"ani-ani-ani-ani-ani-ani aniti me'od"* written throughout with an *alef,* meaning "I have become totally focused on I, myself." The parodic phrase "I, I, I, I, I, I . . . have become only I," is a condemnation of the narcissism from which Gavriella has fled.[69] It might also be pointed out that the conclusion of the prayer intoned by Gavriella is *"ani amarti be-ḥofzi kol ha-adam kozev,"* ("I said in my haste that all men are treacherous"). At least subliminally, this hidden text reflects Gavriella's intense disappointment in seeking genuine love relationships, surely one of the immediate causes precipitating her metamorphosis.

With regard to Gavriella's fleeing the isolating world of words, she writes the following moving statement in her so-called bona fide autobiographical confession. This is a small portion of the much longer manuscript in which Gavriella disguises herself as "Nogah" and refers to Avivit as "Dinah." The smaller section entitled "Life" *("Ḥayyim")* and consisting of a few, very revealing, pages that Avivit discovers concealed in her mother's copy of Dostoevsky's *The Idiot* is printed in its entirety twice[70] in *Persephone Zokheret:*

> There is no salvation in words.
>
> The words that I write do not bring me closer to the world. They divide between me and it. Instead of stripping my skin from off myself and screaming from pain, because that is what I should do, I smear oil on it. Lick myself like a cat.
>
> How beautiful everything is in the words of a poem! What original expressions she has, this poet! Alliterations, connotations. . . .
>
> I can shove them, all of these learned praises.
>
> What does it give me in life, I ask? In life, I ask! Does it free me from depressions? This imaginary glory. Does it free me to get even one inch closer to the outside air? . . . .
>
> My dear husband, my son, my daughter, it doesn't pay, there is so much suffering in the world, and I wrap myself up like a snail in my own shell."[71]

Gavriella even expresses frustration with the enterprise of poetry as a genuine expression of oneself or as a medium of genuine communication. "The language of poetry," she says, "is trained for lying. (*"me'ummenet leshaqqer"*) The more poems are sincere, the very essence of sincerity and truth, so are they more deceitful."[72]

Gavriella/Nogah states that she has "determined to write the story of her life with the clear knowledge that there is no salvation in words."[73] She refers several times in a kind of refrain and with abundant Greek references to her isolation, fears, and vulnerability.[74] The reader is struck by Gavriella's statement as the quintessential artist that she does not enjoy being an outsider, albeit as a superior individual.

For her whole life she has longed for *"achavah,"* a sense of fraternal harmony or belonging:

> "*Achavah, achavah. Ani kemeha le-achavah.* . . . " I yearn for *achavah* . . . Did they think that because of arrogance I wanted to set myself apart from the group? But I wanted to be loved, accepted, one of the group (*achat mikullam*) and it's amazing that even today they think of me as arrogant, and my daughter more than anyone.[75]

Gavriella recalls that even as a young girl in school she experienced fainting spells, presumably as a result of her feelings of alienation. She fell from the "heights of Olympus, where she was immortal (*bat alma-vet*), in the middle of the class."[76] By the word "immortal" Gavriella presumably intends to describe her pronounced feelings of superiority and/or the way, she believed, her peers regarded her.

The Greek references continue.[77] Gavriella awakens at night from the barking of a dog, thinking: "This is Cerberus lying at the gate of Sheol (Hades) and threatening me, not just from today, nor from yesterday. He stalks my soul. He begins with terrifying barks when he only just smells weakness."[78] She believes Cerberus led her to make this impulsive mistake of saying to her husband,

> "I want us to get divorced." This irresponsible impulsiveness. Without any deliberation. Without thinking of the consequences. Did not Orpheus lose Eurydice due to his haste, when he cast his gaze backward when he was ascending from Sheol? Did not Deianira bring death upon herself when she anointed Hercules with a poison instead of a love potion?[79]

These fearful mythological references strengthen the impression not only that Gavriella knows she has made a tragic error in saying she wanted a divorce,[80] but that her mental life has become overwhelmed by the Greek influences she has courted throughout her career. One can also state the matter more plainly: In her longing for love Gavriella had fallen into a state of anomie, accentuated by the Greek model of arbitrary and capricious forces that rule the universe. In this arbitrary Greek world where passions run riot Gavriella repeatedly demeans herself in her search for a romantic relationship. Gavriella's daughter, Avivit, is appalled. When her friend Shuli tells her that "everyone knows" that Gavriella has shamelessly pursued a certain professor of Greek, Avivit is so outraged that, "like the ancient Greeks," Avivit wants to "kill the messenger." Her mother and this world famous authority had been collaborating on the translation of the elegies of some Greek poet. They had an affair, but when he tried to break off the relationship, Gavriella stalked him, disgraced herself and wound up being hospitalized for depression. Avivit cannot believe that her mother the "proud Aristocratic poet," would so demean herself. "On the other hand," [Avivit] tells [herself], "even in the Greek dramas, impulses of jealousy and vengeance change queens into maidservants" in terms of their behavior and their sense of injured pride. Avivit asks: "Had the '*yevaniyyut*' ('the Greek-ness') of this professor so dizzied her mind as to make her lose every drop of self-respect?" Her mother had been hospitalized before with bouts of depression, but this episode had something more to it, something "mythological." Avivit wonders where did she have her trysts with her "Apollo."[81]

What Avivit did not know, until she read the fictionalized autobiography, was that Gavriella had been stalking her divorced former husband as well. Her jealousy of her husband's new romantic relationship was so intense that Gavriella was reduced to hiding in the bushes and spying and fantasizing in the most lurid way about her husband's lovemaking. According to the final chapter of "*Pirqe Nogah*," it appears that Gavriella had become so unnerved by her situation that while shopping in a department store she allowed herself to slip a pair of stockings into her bag without paying for them, and she was then stopped by the store's security guard for shoplifting.

THE ANOMIE OF A GREEK UNIVERSE

Given the plethora of Greek references in *Persephone Zokheret*, it may be speculated that Megged attributes Gavriella's pre-*hitharedut* state of anomie to the contemporary world of sex relations with its chaotic affinity to the pagan world of the Greek gods. Although not perfectly applicable here and perhaps dated, Megged's extremely clever exposition voiced by the bombastic heroine of his 1972 novel *Ha-Hayyim ha-Qesarim*, the redoubtable Elisheva Tal-Blumenfeld, may be relevant here. Elisheva Tal-Blumenfeld contends that the sexual exploits and antics depicted in literature by such authors as Henry Miller are today's "mythology," the equivalent of Homer's depictions of war and violence. For Henry Miller, Elisheva says:

> Sex is like a deity... [sex] is the myth of our day, just as war was the myth of the ancient period, or romantic love—the myth of the days of the [medieval] knights!... [Henry Miller's novels like *Tropic of Cancer*] these are the picaresque novels of our time.... Who is the protagonist who wanders from woman to woman, from bosom to bosom, conquering and not finding his happiness—if not Odysseus of our day, who has lost his cultural assets and is trying to find himself again by means of sexual contact, that in a world devoid of love is the only human contact that is still [possible]?[82]

For all its parodic force in caricaturing a young professorial virtuoso who is carried away with herself, this passage is applicable to the circumstances of Gavriella Gat's life and to the task of deciphering Megged's use of Greek motifs in *Persephone Zokheret*. Gavriella's world is devoid of love, and her perceptions of her sexual encounters—real or imagined, or wished for and unfulfilled—are thoroughly mythicized and ultimately disappointing.

Whether this connection to Megged's 1972 novel and the "sexual mythology" of the 1960s and 1970s is valid or not, Gavriella clearly undergoes a psychological crisis leading up to her "conversion" to Orthodox Judaism. On the threshold of her life change, moreover, Gavriella views her life as if it were in the grip of cosmic mythic forces that threaten to destroy her. It is only in this context that we can understand her behavior as she resorts to Jewish magical incantations, urging herself and talking to herself: "say seven times, *eli, eli atta ḥai ve-go'ali*—say three times: "*qerʿa satan.*"[83]

MEGGED'S AUTHOR PROTAGONISTS IN TORMENT AND TURMOIL

It is telling that in several of his novels Megged tells of authors who became so overwhelmed by the pressures of the literary life that they either contemplated or committed suicide. In *Ha-Gamal ha-Meʿofef ve-Dabbeshet ha-Zahav*, Megged tells the story of the suicides of the authors Avraham Uri Kovner and particularly, of Menachem Mendel Feitelson. Feitelson, a young writer, adored the distinguished author Mendele, but the latter treated him with such utter contempt that this drove Feitelson to suicide.[84] Needless to say, the fictional protagonists of *Ha-Gamal ha-Meʿofef*, particularly the critic Shatz—a composite of Kurzweil[85] and Miron—present a particularly ugly, realistic parody of the Israeli "*republiqah sifrutit,*" as it is often called. Megged lampoons the violence, "carnage," and fear of Israel's literary scene in one especially effective chapter involving Shatz's vitriolic attack on the narrator's poet friend and the unsolved mystery of Shatz being thrown down the staircase of his building and winding up in the hospital.[86]

In *ʿAvel*, of course, Megged depicts a case of literary plagiarism that drives his protagonist Levinstein to self-destruction, but he also recapitulates the tragic end of the Hebrew and Yiddish socialist author Aharon Lieberman.[87] In contemplating his own suicide Levinstein had written letters discussing the suicide of Stavrogin from Dostoevsky's *Devils* and Davidovsky from Brenner's *Mi-Saviv la-Nequdah*.[88] Levinstein's confidante, Beeri, recalls that Levinstein had also spoken about other suicides—Vincent van Gogh, Otto Weininger, Stefan Zweig, and the very interesting case of Cato the Younger. Cato committed suicide because he believed that Julius Caesar was ruining the state, and Dante in his *Divine Comedy*—because this was a suicide based on moral principle—did not consign Cato, along with other committers of suicide, to Hell.[89] Levinstein also had plans to write about three Hebrew authors who died young: Michal, Mane, and Feierberg. Megged's character expresses the notion "that the literary works rise up against their creators"—which is to say, writing is a compulsive activity that can entail enormous pain and sadness. Levinstein coins the phrase "*o ketivuta o mituta*,"[90] one must either write or die," but one is doomed either way.

It is also interesting to note that the central protagonists in such novels as *Mahberot Evyatar, Yom ha-Or shel 'Anat, Dudai'im min ha-Aretz ha-Qedoshah, Foigelman, 'Avel,* and *Persephone Zokheret* each level harsh criticisms at aspects of Israeli culture. The earliest of these protagonists, Richter from Megged's novel of 1982, *Mahberot Evyatar*, is prototypical—almost stereotypical since he is so much more extreme than the protagonists that follow—in his blending of vulnerable ingenuousness, zeal, and caustic self-criticism. We can find some illumination of Megged's portraiture of these complex figures in an article he wrote after giving a ride to an Irish writer who was visiting in Israel.[91] In the literatures of both the Jews and the Irish, Megged writes:

> there are intertwined the cult of the hero and the antihero, the heroic and the antiheroic, and there is a commingling of enthusiasm and irony, and self-mockery; and the greatest zealots are also the greatest sarcastic self-critics.[92]

By Megged's own definition, therefore, the hero is characterized by enthusiasm and zeal, the antihero by self-mockery and sarcasm. Certainly, we can say that Italo Svevo's Zeno is one such antiheroic model for Megged, insofar as the humor is more gentle. By contrast, wherever we find Megged's periodic recourse to the self-lacerating monologue, Dostoevsky's "Man from the Underground" is probably the more apt paradigm.[93]

In *Mahberot Evyatar* Richter is praised at his Jubilee celebration for his quality of "*ahavat yisrael*," love of the Jewish people. Levitin is appalled for he knows the true Richter, and he thinks to himself, "lies, lies."[94] The same Richter who during the 1930s supports the Revisionist line of aggressive retaliation, and writes in the vein of Jabotinsky and Uri Zevi Greenberg about Jewish pride and pedigree, voices what is undoubtedly the most intense diatribe against the behavior of Jews and Zionists that can be found in all of Megged's writings. For sure, in Megged "the greatest zealots are also the greatest sarcastic self-critics." Here is only the smallest sample of Richter's Jewish self-hating remarks:

> Look at the women getting on a bus, being pushed and pushing, sweating, speaking very loud, everything is exposed and open with them, the wide dresses, the vein-protruding legs, the broad thighs, how they pull out their handkerchiefs from their purses, wipe their sweat with a thick crude hand, fanning their faces with it, fanning their knees with the hems of their skirts . . . the lack of any esthetic sense, any natural shyness, any modesty . . . have you seen modesty by us? . . . by us they act brazenly with money, with trickery, now also in governance!

Megged exceeds Hazaz, Mendele, and Brenner in depicting Richter's crescendo of abuse, a catalogue of Jewry's sins that is Rabelaisque in its virtuosity:

> Judaism stinks, Levitin ... *a mile away*, because even its stench it shows off in public, with the same flaunting as with its jewelry! Look all you nations! Look how much better we are than you and be envious! The ten commandments *we* gave to you! Moses and Jesus *we* gave to you! Ethics and wisdom and music and literature, and Spinoza and Freud and Einstein and Rothschild—and *me too*, Morris Sonnenfeld, or Harry Wise, a successful attorney, who struts about now with such boastful pride in the streets of Manhattan, because Freud is mine and Einstein is mine and Rothschild is mine and all of you are worth the skin of a garlic!
>
> I deluded myself that here it is different ... but why is it different? Because here it is organized. We are the legal heirs of the victims of the Shoah for which you are all to blame ... and since righteousness belongs to us and strength belongs to us ... we are *both* the victim *and* the victor. ... We have no sense of mystery. ... Of religion *(dat)* ... yes! But of religiosity *(religiyyah)*? There is no religiosity! Because religiousness is modesty before God! ... The synagogue is a marketplace of peddlers just like the political party and the office and the customs office and the police ... no difference! There they haggle with each other and here they haggle with God, there they yell at one another and here they yell at God! And why—because there is no humility. Because every Jew is as shrewd as God.[95]

Nothing in Megged's latter works—*Yom ha-Or shel 'Anat* or *'Avel* or *Persephone Zokheret*—approaches this sustained diatribe. *'Avel* and *Persephone Zokheret*, in particular, are characterized by greater subtlety. Levinstein in *'Avel* certainly has a much more valid reason than Richter for feeling bitter, and yet he never reaches Richter's level of vitriol. After the shock of seeing his plagiarized poem published, and on the verge of insanity and suicide, Levinstein writes:

> Around me are people of closed-up senses *(atumei ḥushim)*. I see how this opaqueness *(atimut)* is contagious, gradually spreading, with no sense of human contact *(enash be'enash lo pag'a)*. But people revel in this sensory oblivion! They feel good in it! Revelry in Liliput! We are an accursed people Judah, people are at each other's throats, every lowly individual *(nemushah)* delights when he sees the downfall of someone above him; they eat each other up alive. ... I am the son of an accursed people! A base, despised, corrupt people! A people that betrays its destiny, that violates its vows. Everything that the anti-Semites have said about [the Jewish people]—they were right![96]

Levinstein is an enormously conflicted Jewish intellectual. He had been "a great Zionist" and at one point "ostracized" for that. The dilemma of post-1967 Israeli ideology and Megged's own shifting sympathies and polemical battles over some of his unpopular positions may be reflected here. When Levinstein says, for example, that he "loves the Land but to rule over others [he] hates," and then follows this with an outburst, "I am a member of an accursed people!" (*"ani ben le-'am mequllal!*"),[97] it is not so much the specifics as the tenor of this frustrated intellectual's commentary that captures the mood of Megged's own environment from the 1980s until the present. After Levinstein's suicide his friend Be'eri reflects on why Levinstein had been so consumed by his inner torment. Levinstein, he says, did not know how to seek revenge. Be'eri recalls a comment by his own father that we Jews "are a castrated people. Our history and religion have castrated our impulses. We do not know how to avenge. That's it. And he, [Levinstein], too did not know how."[98]

In *Persephone Zokheret*, as well, Gavriella's fictional persona, Nogah, continues in this vein of disenchanted and pained cynicism vis à vis Jewish society. She says that it is easier for her to communicate with people from India, who have a certain naive directness about them. Jews, by contrast, suffer from "an excess of sophistication."[99] Of course, from time to time Gavriella realizes that the fault lies also within herself, and not only with her fellow Israelis and their environment. If she finds it easier to get along with people who are not from her own country, Gavriella reasons during a moment of objectivity, it is "because they don't know her."[100] In a series of chapters that provide the immediate background for Nogah/Gavriella's need to escape from the Israeli secular environment, she writes: "I must become purified." Intensely, she feels "longings for another state of being *(ḥavvayah aḥeret)*." In a more refined environment such as that described in the Chekhov play, "Three Sisters," Gavriella muses, even the sadness is more refined, more "aristocratic" than here, in secular Israel, wherein

> all of the delicate sensibilities are muddied and trampled on by the loudness *(tsa'aqanut)* from which there is no escape. The vulgarity that permeates every corner, the wild political bickering that erupts from out of the television screens, the nervy answers of the male and female clerks, the venom of the newspapers, the arrogant manner of speaking in the street, in the office, and everything, everything is so externalized, *(hakol muḥtsan)*—not a moment of quiet; it seems that people never look inside themselves and ponder.[101]

Nogah/Gavriella longs for the quiet and ascetic, "holy," meditativeness that she finds not only in Chekhov but also in the atmosphere of the Second Aliyah, as depicted in a short story by Zvi Shatz and in the poetry of Raḥel. Perhaps, she muses, she, Nogah/Gavriella, is a reincarnation of Raḥel, and all of her present life has been but a metempsychotic exile from her real, pure self. I would submit that there is not a great psychological distance—not at all a big leap—between Gavriella's identification with the Second Aliyah ethos of "priestly" self-purification and her espousal of the Tsefat *ḥaredi* environment. Both ideals are ascetic, cultic, and mystical. Gavriella/Nogah, in fact, views the ethos of contemporary Tsefat as a continuation of the sixteenth-century kabbalistic sects that were based in this same area.[102]

The "purification" Gavriella longs for is a sea-change, not only from her obsessive searching for romance after her divorce, but from the complete absence in her life, even before the divorce, of any moral and ideological anchor. There are numerous examples of this capricious and ego-driven restlessness. Avivit describes how Gavriella was invited to a conference on "Mediterranean culture"—part of which dealt with Persephone and Tammuz—because of the many Greek references in her poetry. By Avivit's construction, Gavriella had felt so flattered by the attention shown to her, that she facilely espoused this anti-Zionist Mediterranean perspective without having any true ideological understanding of it.[103] Similarly, Gavriella contends that the Arab men she had met, unlike the Israeli men, possess "true gentlemanliness," thereby eliciting an angry response from Avivit's husband Alex. Alex quipped snidely that Gavriella's "thanks" for her "altruistic humanism" could easily be her being gang-raped and then killed by the Arab "gentlemen" who had so impressed her.[104]

Then later, upon the occasion of another Mediterranean culture conference, this one in Israel, Gavriella recklessly went off gallivanting with a musician from Tangiers, thereby worrying Avivit to death.[105] And finally, Gavriella's enthusiasm about seeing Israel as part of "Mediterranean" culture reaches its absurd climax in her expression of empathy for the Palestinian suicide bomber. This family "soap opera," as Avivit described it, leads to Gavriella's husband becoming so irate that, as noted, their already shaky marriage ends in divorce. Megged suggests a possible foreshadowing of Gavriella's total self-absorption during her pampered childhood in the episode of her family's flight to America. The twelve-year-old Gavriella has, or feigns,[106] a panic attack during the flight. On her account the plane has to make an emergency landing in Athens, causing a delay that forces her father to miss his conference in Arizona, and thus ruins the family's vacation—something for which she feels "guilt [her] entire life." But only a year later she flies back to Athens alone and recalls *"sham ra'iti or,"* ("there I saw light,") presumably establishing her lifelong enchantment with Greek culture that was to come at the expense of her family life, human relations, and national allegiances[107]

AFTERWORD AND OVERVIEW:
TENSION BETWEEN THE HERO AND THE ANTIHERO

The following remarks extend beyond the defined bounds of this paper to encompass, albeit tentatively, questions of Megged's vacillation between his respect for positive heroes as "winners" and his regard for antiheroes as "losers." In Megged there is a constant tension between the cult of the hero and of the antihero. I do not believe that Megged ever achieves a wholehearted espousal of the antihero ideal, as, for example, in Shalom Aleichem's glorification of the gallant orphan in *Motel the Cantor's Son* or Hasek's *Good Soldier Schweik*. Megged's Shlomik in *Ḥedvah va-Ani*, comes closest to being a pleasant "schlemiel," who also makes a statement about the devaluation of Zionist values, but he is far from happy. Shlomik becomes the victim of a commercially driven newly bourgeois society. In a more "Kafkaesque" mode, the antihero protagonist of *Miqreh ha-Kesil* assumes, at best, the posture of a figure out of Mendele, a misfit who lives a passable life but is never content and cannot be considered a healthy archetype. Megged's other "schlemiel" antihero types, Michah Shtoq (1986)[108] and Asa'el, also end up very badly, and I have serious doubts as to the positive resolution of the malaise and ennui of virtually all his antiheroes, including the literary antihero types dealt with in this paper.

From the postscript to Shlomik's story in *Ha-Gamal ha-Me'ofef*, we see that from Megged's perspective, every iota of humor has been drained out of the Hedvah and Shlomik story.[109] Equally, it strikes one as sad that even in the highly humorous *Ha-Gamal ha-Me'ofef*, satire has gained the upper hand over humor. Similarly, if we compare the figure of Afarsemon in *Ḥedvah va-Ani* with a protagonist of the later story, "Michah Shtoq" (1986), we find there an unsavory character of a similar but darker cast, Avraham (Avrum) Erlich. Avrum, like Afarsemon, is a careerist who has betrayed the ideals of 1948. But in "Michah Shtoq" one detects our author's far greater degree of antipathy. The personality profile of this "smooth operator type" is more complex, more hypocritical, and more insidious. During the 1948 campaign Avrum had conveniently absented himself from the field of battle, at a time when Michah was in desperate straits, and as a result he suffered the strangely debilitating wounds that rendered him incapable of forgetting anything. He was prone to violent rages. If Shlomik just walks off into the sunset, Michah delivers justice with a strong hand, killing Mr. Avrum.

The following is a partial hypothesis to explain the relentless unhappy endings meted out to Megged's antiheroes. For all of Megged's acclamation of Yiddish culture and his "fondness"[110] for the antihero, Megged may not be fully capable of assimilating as a positive hero the Jewish *galut* stereotype of the weak and emotional "good man," as the philosopher Ernst Simon referred to it in one of his rare articles on Israeli literature. Of course, many of his heroes are "outsiders" or nonconformists. This has nothing to do with the *galut* (except insofar as many Jewish *galut* intellectuals perceived themselves this way), but for the moment I wish to highlight the issue of strength and success or winning. Megged's heroes remain in limbo, if not in purgatory. The case of *Foigelman*, is, of course, the most obvious. A sabra historian sets out to assist and reclaim for Hebrew culture its lost component, but it is obvious, practically from the outset, that Megged "cannot go home again." The poet Shmuel Foigelman notes that the fate of Yiddish literary ventures is akin to that of "Peter Shlemiehl who is cut off from his shadow."[111] It is curious that utilizing this same ambiguously engaging metaphor many years earlier, the philosopher Ernst Simon had characterized the protagonist in *Miqreh ha-Kesil*—a protagonist left nameless and thus, according to Simon, rendered by Megged "even less a person" than Kafka's K.–as symbolic of "a lost generation." The "Kesil," said Simon, was hence comparable to "Peter Shlemiehl, the person bereft of a shadow."[112]

The very reference to this precursor of the Jewish appropriation of the word "schlemiel" is most provocative, and it does indeed capture the sense of existential angst suggested by Chamisso's tale. It does not, however, automatically define a particular protagonist as a "schlemiel" in the sense of being a hapless simpleton. A more apt and helpful simile may be available to us from Shmuel Foigelman's long excursus on Don Quixote and his assertion that he would want to write a novel about Don Quixote's horse, Rosinante, particularly as this horse appears, crying, in the painting by Daumier. Foigelman would compare Rosinante to Mendele's "*Susati*" as a symbol both of himself and of the Jewish people. Foigelman clearly sees himself embodied in this horse who "carries his demented rider from town to town . . . receiving blows and curses, wounded in the wars with windmills and all kinds of wayfarers, decent and crooked, and not knowing why all of these things come upon him . . . "[113] In the end, no doubt in keeping with the Yiddish poet's image of himself as transcending fate through his "bird-like" courage and sensibilities, Foigelman says he would have his equine protagonist sprout wings, so that the horse could soar, not like Pegasus, but, again, rather like a winged version of Mendele's "Susati."[114]

The question of physical courage and the need for the Jew in his own land to protect himself seems to be so deeply ingrained in Megged that he cannot fully glorify the weak individual. Megged's famous chapter "Ha-'Ir ha-Levanah" in *Miqreh ha-Kesil* comes closest to dignifying an act of conscience by the nameless protagonist who refuses to kill a young Arab during the 1956 Sinai campaign. But even in that work of Megged, following what for him was the most problematic of Israel's wars,[115] and writing a satirical novel that most closely approximates an anti-war spoof, Megged does not come down squarely on the side of the pacifists. The well-known pacifist philosopher and educator, Ernst Simon, might have wished for Megged to do this. Simon, who clearly appreciated Megged's posing of ethical dilemmas, may have been incorrect in his insinuation that, because Megged cites from St. Augustine on the front page of the novel, Megged's dilemma stems from his unwillingness to consult Jewish ethical sources. Perhaps, by Simon's lights, this illustrates Megged's unwillingness to justify passive resistance and/or insubordination.[116] The novel *Miqreh ha-Kesil* was ambiguous enough to situate Megged's *"kesil"* in the avant-garde of the agonizing peace camp[117] together, as Simon said, with "his spiritual blood relative," [the Israeli officer] who did not free the *"shavui"*[118] ("The Captive"), in Yizhar's famous short story of that name. It seems to me that Megged does not disavow the appropriate use of violence in military operations. Admittedly, it is B., the former officer of "The Society of the Wicked," who says: "Only the fool is of the opinion that righteousness and weakness came into this world intertwined."[119] Nevertheless, this prosecutorial comment leveled against the *"kesil"* possesses the ring of an ineluctable truth, as far as Megged is concerned. The moral citizen of Israel is not free to desist from necessary violence in war. The most that we can say is that the hero takes flight from his ethical impasse in a grotesque manner by virtue of the otherworldly conclusion of the novel in the form of "a trial of the dead" followed by the protagonist's psychic return visit to the moshav of his youth.

Part of Megged's dilemma is that he is uneasy with both the old *galut* stereotype of the passive Jew and the new stereotype of the Israeli as a macho *"chevreman"* and *"matzlichan,"* a back-slapping careerist and opportunist. The conflict with regard to the *galut* stereotype is prominent first in *Maḥberot Evyatar* and then again in *Foigelman*. In both of these novels a real-life traumatic episode experienced by Megged is starkly foreshadowed. Our author filters through the mouths of Richter in the former novel and Arbel in the latter novel the enduring impact of a trip Megged took as a teenager to Trumpeldor's shrine in the Galilee in 1937.[120] The fictional accounts do not exaggerate Megged's feeling of shame and cowering before an angry Arab mob, his embarrassed shock at having been through a "pogrom," and his visceral unwillingness to believe the possibility of Jewish powerlessness *within* Israel. Megged's interview of 1973 confirms the factuality of these accounts.[121] In *Maḥberot Evyatar* the narrator notes the paradox that Richter, for all his ideological espousal of a right-wing militant position, was himself, physically, a coward. In this instance he was cringing in a restaurant in Tiberias.[122] In *Foigelman* the sabra historian Arbel feels "tears choking his throat, tears of shame and insult, and although British soldiers arrived to disperse the crowd of Arabs, Arbel indicates, "the memory of that disgrace has not been erased from [his] heart."[123]

Brombert offers an interesting hypothesis with regard to Svevo's Zeno that casts light on the tensions pervading Megged's protagonists. "Self-abasement," Brombert writes, "is dialectically bound up with the awareness of the admired model. The antihero can exist only if the heroic model remains present in absentia, by preterition,"[124]—i.e., by self-conscious omission. Svevo lists a whole series of virile and victorious types: "Napoleon, Don Juan, the heroes of mythology, Oedipus...," who he admires in his own creative way. If his psychiatrist expects Zeno to feel "sick" when he presents him with the diagnosis of "the Oedipus Complex "... Zeno deconstructs the Freudian interpretation in order to reinstate the dignity of suffering. Zeno claims to be delighted because the Oedipus complex elevates him to "the highest nobility." Oedipus for Zeno is Sophocles' hero who "has the courage to pursue truth and to discover (and uncover) himself."[125]

For Megged, too, mutatis mutandis, the model of strength in battle and heroic self-sacrificing labor for the sake of the collective is ever present by virtue of his upbringing and education. It is my speculation that Megged would at no time renounce the ideal of the true Zionist hero: one who is strong, self-sacrificing, not self-indulgent, considerate of others (foremost among whom would be the hero's own family), possessed of both national and universal vision, and of a keen moral barometer. At one point in my correspondence with Megged he wrote to me that Yigal Allon had been something of a heroic figure for him, perhaps something of an ideal. Even the composite figure behind Davidov in *Ha-Ḥai 'al ha-Met*—be it Yitzḥaq Sadeh or any number of complex and "imperfect" individuals like him—remains, I believe, the object of Megged's veneration.

Although we cannot be sure if the following eloquent opinion on the topic of heroes in the modern age, as expressed by one protagonist in a novel, is identical to that of Megged or not, it is worth citing in the present context:

> Is the writing of a heroic epic possible in the modern era? This is a period in Israel and in the world of "the murder of heroes," both from the distant past and the recent past. And if they do not murder them they make them into dwarfs *(megammedim otam)*, so that their stature should not, God forbid, be higher than every... average person. Since most people are inclined today to live for the moment, in a comfortable and serene way, and they do not have ideals or goals for which it is worthwhile to sacrifice one's life, then consciously or unconsciously they cast doubt on the very possibility of the existence of this trait—"heroism" in the life of Man...[126]

At least part of Megged shares in Levinstein's lament. In *Ga'agu'im le-Olga,* by sharp contrast, our author registers a plea for the unexceptional individual, the person who feels "alienated" from the group, and for whom articulate self-expression is difficult. "*Ashrei 'ilge ha-lashon....* " "Lucky are the awkward of speech, the stammerers, the halting ones, whose speech is not polished, not overbearing, for theirs is the kingdom of heaven."[127] Megged maintains the coexistence of and tension between the cult of the hero and the antihero. These contradictory attractions stem in part from Megged's staunch Zionist leanings, his admiration for heroism and self-sacrifice, and his equally strong desire to reclaim the less "macho" and perhaps more "feminine" cultural and emotional legacy of the *golah*. His choice of feminine protagonists in several of his recent novels may be indicative of this thrust. At the same time quite apart from the *eretz yisrael* versus *golah* dichotomy, Megged demonstrates an intrinsic affinity for shyness and reserve in the face of stereotypical sabra braggadocio; and for privacy and individualistic taste in the face of what he sees as an Israeli penchant for group activity and conformity to peer pressure. This dichotomous and paradoxical allegiance to the hero and the antihero at one and the same time produces a tension within Megged—and perhaps within Jewish culture as a whole.

HEBREW UNION COLLEGE–JEWISH INSTITUTE OF RELIGION, N.Y.C.

NOTES

1. Aharon Megged, *Persephone Zokheret* (Tel Aviv, 2000). Megged's fine interview about this novel with *Ha-Aretz* Neri Livneh ("Massa Eḥad," June 29, 2000), came to my attention only when I completed this article. Megged then also sent me a copy of his latest novel, *'Ad ha-'Erev* (Tel Aviv, 2001) that, in his words, "constitutes one more level" in this topic of the antihero.

2. Megged, *Ha-Ḥai 'al ha-Met* (Tel Aviv, 1965).

3. Megged, *Maḥberot Evyatar* (Tel Aviv, 1982).

4. Megged, *Foigelman* (Tel Aviv, 1987).

5. Megged, *Persephone Zokheret*, p. 228. Gavriella names her daughter Avivit in memory of her first love, a boy named Aviv (the Hebrew word for Spring), who dies in battle, but also as a clear evocation of the springtime motif and the goddess Persephone.

6. See, for example, ibid., pp. 63, 225, 231.

7. Ibid., pp. 185–186.

8. Victor Brombert, *In Praise of Antiheroes* (Chicago, 1999).

9. See Megged, "Shesh Nefashot Mehappesot Motsa," from the version originally in *Moznayim*, Vol. XXIII, Nos. 1-2 (Sivan-Tammuz, 1966); henceforth cited as "Shesh Nefashot" in *Shulḥan ha-Ketivah* (Tel Aviv, 1989), p. 77. Writing about Gogol's "The Nose," Dostoevsky's "The Double," and Kafka's "Metamorphosis," Megged declares: "This plebeian dynasty—made up of petty bureaucrats, traveling salesmen, clerks, *lo-yutzlachim* ("losers"), *bene beli shem* ("nameless or unremarkable types")—refutes, as it were, Aristotle's claim that tragedy imitates people of a type superior to the usual and comedy imitates people of a type lower than the usual. Gogol . . . Svevo . . . and their offspring have made the ordinary into the dominant, and shown that it contains something of the

profoundly tragic, as well as something of the profoundly comic, and of both at the same time."

10. Defined in a standard English dictionary as "an awkward and unlucky person for whom things never turn out right." Also see infra, n. 112. The *Universal Jewish Encyclopedia* defines "schlemiel" as one who "handles a situation in the worst possible manner or is dogged by an ill luck that is more or less due to his own ineptness" (cited by Sanford Pinsker in *The Schlemiel as Metaphor* [London, 1971], p. 5).

11. Megged, ʻAsaʼel (Tel Aviv, 1978) and see, for example, A. B. Yafeh, "Mi-Shlumiʼel ʻad ʻAsaʼel," *Yediʻot Aḥaronot* (January 12, 1979). Yafeh begins with a discussion of Shelumiel/Schlemiel.

12. Megged, *Gaʻaguʻim le-Olga* (Tel Aviv, 1994), p. 25.

13. Ibid., p. 25. Albert states that he feels even less important than Akaky Akakievich from Gogol's famous story "The Overcoat." This classic nonperson was able to leave his "mark," Albert reasons, through his distinctive penmanship. The computer robs one even of this ability to rise above anonymity.

14. See Megged, "Ha-Meshorer ve-ha-Qesar, *Ha-Aretz* (June 26, 1987); and in Megged's *Shulḥan ha-Ketivah* (Tel Aviv, 1989), pp. 42–45. In responding to criticisms of Amos Oz's novel *Qufsah Sheḥorah,* Megged cites the paradox that humanist authors such as Gogol and Dostoevsky had reactionary views. He is surprised that politicians seek authors' opinions in Israel, and cites many negative characteristics of authors (and artists) as a group, and why it is unwise to solicit their political opinions: "They are most unstable by their very nature, changeable, egocentric, often lying and traitorous with regard to things outside of their creativity, flattering, 'ready to sell their mothers,' as long as they can achieve recognition, a good word; and because they possess what Keats calls 'negative talent'—the talent to be skeptical of truths and to live in uncertainty. Furthermore, their principal interest is in the human psyche with all of its polarities, and not in the administration of the state." Megged cites a dialogue from H. G. Welles's novel: "What you seek in men of letters is a sensitive nervous constitution, quick responses to stimuli, an alert, almost unrestrained, expressiveness... do you imagine for a moment that these qualities lead to self-control, to sober judgment, consistency, to everything that makes a person reliable? No, we are not consistent, our good qualities are our deficiencies." Also see Megged's comment that uncovering the biography of an author can be quite distressing (in "Ha-Banaliyyut shel ha-Sevel—62 Shanah le-Moto shel Franz Kafka," *Ha-Aretz* [June 6, 1986]; and in Megged, *Shulḥan ha-Ketivah,* pp. 84–87). Also, Megged's *Maḥberot Evyatar,* pp. 16–17; therein a member of the committee that decides to publish all four volumes of the material on Richter, warts and all, cites "Sigmund Freud in his famous essay on Leonardo da Vinci, [who] writes that biographers who write an idealized version of their hero, erase from his portrait the traces of his life struggle externally and internally, and conceal his weaknesses; thereby they impart to him a cold and alien image and miss the opportune moment that they had to penetrate the most amazing secrets of human nature." In the same paragraph we find this comment: "Had an artistic genius like Dostoevsky been judged only according to the testimonies of his contemporaries who were close to him, perhaps he would have been consigned to Hell, but we know that he merited Eternity." On Byron see

Megged's *Yom ha-Or shel 'Anat* (Tel Aviv, 1992), p. 209. See also the citation from Shakespeare's *A Midsummer's Night Dream* (*Yom ha-Or shel 'Anat*, p. 155) that there are three types of people whose imaginations drive them to insanity: the madman, the lover, and the poet.

15. See the conversation with Hedvah in Megged's *Ha-Gamal ha-Me'ofef ve-Dabbeshet ha-Zahav* (Tel Aviv, 1982), pp. 118–119 (henceforth, *Ha-Gamal ha-Me'ofef*). For the record, it should be stated that Megged does not himself specifically define the flawed creative artist as an antihero. This is our own addition to this complex subject.

16. Megged, *Persephone Zokheret*, pp. 244, 248. In her fictional "diaries," Gavriella transparently refers to herself as "Nogah" and to her daughter Avivit as "Dinah."

17. Ibid., p. 231. Also p. 248.

18. Avivit writes that the play she directs about Hannah and Her Seven Sons may have been her "war against the 'Hellenization' of [her] mother." Ibid., p. 33. Avivit is also active in an organization to fight against the domination of non-Hebraic words, (Ibid., p. 43) an activity worthy of a latter-day disciple of S. D. Luzzatto. Avivit also speculates that precisely because her mother kept her knowledge of classical Jewish texts to herself and used them as "seasoning" in her poems, Avivit had become curious to find out more about Jewish sources (Ibid., p. 45).

19. Ibid., p. 190.

20. On Luzzatto's dichotomy between Judaism and Hellenism see Shalom Spiegel, *Hebrew Reborn* (Philadelphia, 1962), pp. 87–90.

21. Megged, *Persephone Zokheret*, p.158.

22. See Megged's short entry "Ḥibbah la-Anti-Gibbor" in "Mish'al: Ha-Tovim be-Sifre TaSHMaZ," *Ha-Aretz* (September 23, 1987). He cites a work by Robert Walser "'*Ozer le-Khol 'Et*" Walser's hero, Megged says, is "less enigmatic than [Kafka]'s K. . . . but Yozef is clearer than [K.], easier than he and one who wins our empathy by virtue of several similar qualities. A man who stands on the margins of society, whom 'life neglects' as he says of himself." . . . "By contrast to the tragic sarcasm of Kafka, Walser's stories are permeated with the humor of resignation. In this short response to a reporter's query Megged also cites Joseph Roth's antihero "Trotte" in *The Radetsky March*, or Zeno of Svevo, and Agnon's Herschel in *Sippur Pashut*.

23. Supra, n. 5.

24. In Megged's *Ha-Ḥayyim ha-Qeṣarim* (Tel Aviv, 1972), p. 47, Elisheva Tal-Blumenfeld cites Max Frisch's novel *Homo Faber* together with Herzog, Durrenmat, and Henry Miller as examples of great contemporary world literature that deal not only with reportage but with "La condition humaine." He also cites Frisch in "Miqreh Avraham ben-Avraham (Yomano shel Ezrah)," *Davar* (March 5, 1976), p. 11. Megged read about an Arab who was a convert to Judaism who was being unfairly treated after his wife reconverted back to Islam. Megged goes to visit this *ger-tzedek*. Megged compares this situation to Max Frisch's work, "Andora" and to Shofman's stories about Jews in Austrian villages.

25. Kenaz, Yehoshu'a. "Le-Va'ayat ha-Sippur she-Lo Nikhtav" *La-Merḥav*, April 16, 1965. Kenaz suggests that Megged's Jonas is influenced by Camus's

hero of the same name (in Albert Camus, "The Artist at Work" in *The Exile and the Kingdom* [New York, 1972], pp. 110-158). Moreover, Camus introduces his story with a quote from the biblical book of Jonah.

26. Megged, "Shesh Nefashot," *Shulhan ha-Ketivah*, pp. 76-77.

27. Ibid., p. 54. Jonah's is "an absurd flight but one that is understood as a wish; either to a state of nonbeing, of a fetus in its mother's womb, like the flight into the belly of the ship, into the intestines of the fish, to the shelter of the *qiqqayon* (the gourd) in the desert. . . . "Its only outlet," as Megged writes earlier (p. 52), "is flight from reality in its entirety, a flight that assumes a grotesque or fantastic character, and that, per force, has no solution. It ends with a sigh or with a question mark." Megged sees Jonah as the archetype of the "alienated man" (*"haadam hamenukkar"*) as opposed to Kierkegaarde's (and perhaps Abraham's and Job's) ability to bless the silence of God—see pp. 55-56. Jonah and a long series of "antiheroes" who follow after him "found the ability to ask" about the silence of God, but not the ability to bless this silence. Jonah's story is the only one in the Bible to end in a question mark.

28. Meyer Levin, *National Jewish Post and Opinion* (Indianapolis), October 12, 1962.

29. Cf. reference to Tal-Blumenfeld in Megged, *Ha-Gamal ha-Me'ofef*, p. 61. In *Ha-Gamal ha-Me'ofef* Megged also brings together some characters from Megged's earlier novels such as Hedvah from *Hedvah va-Ani* and Heinz from *Heinz Hirsch u-Veno ve-ha-Ru'ah ha-Ra'ah*—both residents in the protagonist's building. It should also be pointed out that the protagonist of *Ha-Gamal ha-Me'ofef* was working on a translation of Rabelais (cf. Bakhtin, infra, n. 41.) The subversive nature of the carnivalesque, according to Bakhtin, is by now very well known. For Megged it may have been primarily an opportunity to demonstrate his linguistic virtuosity.

30. Megged, *Yom ha-Or shel 'Anat* (Tel Aviv, 1992). There is also some similarity to the motif in Megged's very early novella "Massa'a el Eretz Gomer," in Megged, *Ha-Berihah* (Tel Aviv, 1962), pp. 69-146. There he depicts a society, a parody of the Soviet Union, totally overwhelmed by materialism, in which "no one dreams." I lectured on this theme at the NAPH convention in Toronto in May 1992, a paper that is not yet published.

31. Megged, *Duda'im min ha-Aretz ha-Qedoshah* (Tel Aviv, 1998). On this novel see my article, "Patterns of Failed Return in Aharon Megged's Work: Revisiting the Jewish-Christian Nexus," *Modern Judaism*, Vol. 19 (1999), pp. 277-292.

32. See "Shesh Nefashot" *Shulhan ha-Ketivah*, p. 53. By contrast, the professor and literary critic Elisheva Tal-Blumenfeld in Megged's much earlier *Ha-Hayyim ha-Qesarim* (Tel Aviv, 1972), who is reincarnated in *Ha-Gamal ha-Me'ofef*, is so much the caricature of an aggressive and bombastic female professional that it is hard to characterize her as resembling the far more vulnerable female types in Megged's recent novels.

33. See my article, "Patterns of Failed Return," *Modern Judaism*, n. 31.

34. Megged, *Yom ha-Or shel 'Anat*, p. 66.

35. Ibid., p. 197.

36. Ibid. Cf. the figure of 'Asa'el in Megged's novel, supra, n. 11. According to Hillel Weiss "'Asa'el," *Ma'ariv* (April 13, 1979), the novel reflects Meg-

ged's longing for a reality that tolerates the quiet suffering type and poses a skeptical challenge to the "*matzlichan*," the hard-driving, and success-oriented type.

37. Megged, *Yom ha-Or shel 'Anat*, pp. 90, 194–197.

38. Ibid., p. 170.

39. See Megged's interview article with Shulamit Lan entitled "Anahnu Shoqe'im be-Refesh 'ad Ṣavvar" in *Ha-Aretz* (June 19, 1992), pp. 7–8.

40. The reviewer Iyze Perliss (in "Ben Masoret le-Hilloniyyut," *Ha-Do'ar*, Vol. 79, No. 21 [September 29, 2000], pp. 32–33) makes far too much of Megged's negation of Israeli secular culture. Surely, Perliss can not believe that Megged intends to present the *ḥaredi* lifestyle as a viable option. Gavriella's bizarre transformation is simply one form of the pattern of grotesque flight from an intolerable reality that is typical of Megged's antiheroic protagonists.

41. See Mikhail Bakhtin, *Rabelais and His World* (Bloomington, 1984). And see Megged's comment in "Shesh Nefashot": "Tragedy imitates people of a type superior to the usual and Comedy imitates people of a type lower than the usual. Gogol . . . Svevo . . . and their offspring have made the usual dominant and shown that it contains something of the profoundly tragic and the profoundly comic, and of both at the same time."

42. Megged, *Yom ha-Or shel 'Anat*, pp. 26–33.

43. Ibid., pp. 21, 74, 115, 171–173.

44. Megged, *Persephone Zokheret*, p. 108. Cf. the remarks of Evyatar Levitin in Megged, *Maḥberot Evyatar*, p. 116: "I was with them in their [bed]rooms, into their souls I peeked through the latticework of the letters, I saw them in their love-making, their pleasures, with the language, the words, the plots, *the substance of life*, in their mighty masculine conquests—and I served them . . . yes, like a eunuch I served them . . . " One recalls, of course, the theme of the envy of Mozart's artistic greatness in the play "Amadeus," a theme that goes backs to Pushkin.

45. Megged, *Persephone Zokheret*, p. 113.

46. Ibid., p. 49.

47. Ibid., pp. 207–208.

48. Ibid., p. 91.

49. Ibid., p. 99.

50. Ibid., p. 231.

51. Ibid.

52. Ibid., p. 97.

53. V. Brombert, *In Praise of Antiheroes*, p. 90. Brombert juxtaposes *Homo Faber* with *Homo Ludens* (playful, speculative, artistic man). See also Megged, *Persephone Zokheret*, p. 84.

54. Megged writes in praise of Erasmus and his "In Praise of Folly" in *Ha-Ḥayyim ha-Qeṣarim*," pp. 108–109.

55. Megged, *Miqreh ha-Kesil* (Tel Aviv, 1959) and see Menahem Brinker, "Ha-Ḥalusiyyut ba-'Am u-ve-Sifrutenu ha-Ṣe'irah," *Mibifnim* (February, 1954), pp. 381–391, who notes the virtual absence of humor in current Israeli literature. Megged alone developed it, Brinker said, after the writing of *Ru'aḥ Yammim* (Tel Aviv, 1949).

56. In *Ha-Gamal ha-Me'ofef*, Megged's most fully developed work of parody, he traces his protagonist's becoming a Zionist to his meeting with a Hebrew author (Megged himself), who in August and September of 1953 came as a young man to an international communist youth festival in Rumania. This festival, that was for the real-life Megged the height of his Marxist involvement, is now transformed into the site of origin of Megged's most uproarious spoof, *Ha-Gamal ha-Me'ofef*.

57. Megged, *Foigelman*, p. 243.

58. Megged, *Persephone Zokheret*, p. 218 (in the chapter entitled "Unicorn"): After recalling that she had forgotten to call to say goodbye to her daughter Nogah/Gavriella writes: "... when she calls me she never begins with Hello Mother, but rather a curt hello, with pursed lips. Yes, there are thorns beneath her tongue."

59. This is a summary of the legend by V. Brombert in *In Praise of Antiheroes*, p. 93.

60. From Edith Hamilton, *Mythology* (New York, 1998), pp. 63–64. "In the stories of both goddesses, Demeter and Persephone, the idea of sorrow was foremost. Demeter, goddess of the harvest wealth, was still more the divine sorrowing mother who saw her daughter die each year. Persephone was the radiant maiden of the spring and the summertime ... but all the while Persephone knew how brief that beauty was; fruit, flowers, leaves, all the fair growth of earth, must end with the coming of the cold and pass like herself into the power of death. After the lord of the dark world below carried her away she was never again the gay young creature who had played in the flowery meadow without a thought of care or trouble. She did indeed rise from the dead every spring, but she brought with her the memory of where she had come from; with all her bright beauty there was something strange and awesome about her. She was often said to be 'the maiden whose name may not be spoken.' The Olympians were 'the happy gods' ... far removed from suffering mortals destined to die. But in their grief and at the hour of death, men could turn for compassion to the goddess who sorrowed and the goddess who died." (pp. 63–64).

61. In each of these novels, mention of the fictional novel's title is only tangential: in Megged's *Persephone Zokheret* this happens to be the title of Gavriella's first book of poetry. In his *Yom ha-Or shel 'Anat* this happens to be the title of a book by the invited showpiece guest to 'Anat's wedding, a secondary character at best.

62. See his "Ha-Sofer ke-Pygmalion," *Moznayim* (August-September, 1975), pp.163–169; and in Megged's *Shulḥan ha-Ketivah*, pp. 24–34. Coincidentally, one of Megged's quotations at the beginning of a chapter is from the section of Ovid's *Metamorphoses* entitled "Pygmalion." See Megged, *Persephone Zokheret*, p. 230. For another reference to this story see page 260. Nogah muses about the young woman in the studio of the artist with whom she wishes to become romantic: "Perhaps she is his Galatea." In this article Megged cites the speech of Shylock as an example of the way an author changes his feelings towards a protagonist. Megged says that it is not an accident that Ovid made Pygmalion into a sculptor and not a painter (Ibid., p. 27). In this more extended process,

"through the magic of the alchemy of the creative process, which is esthetic, [the ugly] itself becomes so beautiful that one can fall in love with it."

63. See Zelda's poem "Ki ha-Or Sha'ashu'ai," *Shire Zelda* (Tel Aviv, 1985), pp. 87–88.

64. Megged, *Persephone Zokheret*, p. 198.

65. Cf. A. B. Yehoshua, *Ha-Me'ahev* (Tel Aviv, 1977) and in English translation, *The Lover* (New York, 1985). See *Mass'a be-Av* (Tel Aviv, 1984) and my article "Aharon Megged's Burden in His Depiction of the Aftermath of Israel's Wars" forthcoming in the *Arnold Band Jubilee Volume*.

66. *Persephone Zokheret*, p. 79.

67. Ibid., p. 228. Gavriella identifies with the line in *Hamlet* addressed to Ophelia, "get thee to a nunnery."

68. On some level, Megged's mother, although she was not religious, may have served as a model for the altered Gavriella and for the chauvinistic aspects of Avivit. In "Ishah Yehudiyyah," *Monitin* (February, 1981), pp. 126–127, Megged notes that his mother used to do things that would embarrass him. She would go in uninvited and teach Hasidic songs to a group of young people who were having a party. Equally, his mother was a fanatic for Hebrew purism. Megged's mother more evidently served as a model for the eponymous hero in Megged's novel *Asahel* (Tel Aviv, 1978).

69. See Megged, *Persephone Zokheret*, pp. 184, 187. Previously, Gavriella intones the first part of the prayer: "*'odecha ki 'anitani, va-tehi li liyeshu'ah*" (p. 157).

70. Ibid., pp. 191–198 and 285–288. The fictional editor of the two parts of the novel brings these pages once as part of Avivit's descriptive remarks and a second time as part of Gavriella/Nogah's total "diaries."

71. Ibid., pp. 193 and 287.

72. Ibid., p. 158.

73. Ibid., p. 193.

74. In a kind of stream-of-consciousness writing Gavriella gives vent to her neurotic fears, incanting–"words words" like a refrain: "What are we talking about, after all. Words words. But words last longer than deeds, said the Greeks." (220) She speaks of her many fears: fear of holes, the hole in the ozone, the hole of the woman's cervix in her father's gynecological clinic, and the fear of death as a kind of black hole, ending again with "words words." See ibid., pp. 218, 220, 224, 225.

75. Ibid., p. 226. In a section from Gavriella's bona fide autobiography (presented twice in the two discrete sections of the novel), Avivit's recounting and Gavriella's material, pp. 192 and 285, Gavriella's writes: "How does it happen that my absolute, ultimate loneliness is interpreted by people as snobbishness?" At one point Avivit says that even she herself had felt this "unfilled longing for love" from reading Gavriella's first book, *Persephone Zokheret*.

76. Megged, *Persephone Zokheret*, p.228.

77. Among the many other Greek references: after meeting the Dane, Jalmar, Gavriella/Nogah says she is "a complete failure, that [she] has lived with half a soul, as a cripple, because [she] has not joined up with [her] second half." This is an allusion to the mythic statement of Aristophanes in Plato's *Symposium*. She also thinks of being in bed with the Dane, who, like a young

Greek, "like Glaucus who rules the oceans will penetrate into her, forge into the depths" (Ibid., p. 240). Following her rejection by the Dane, Gavriella writes a poem containing the line *"en almugim be-Hades"* ("there are no corals in Hades" p. 65). Avivit gave up the chance to study natural sciences, in which she excelled. Out of a desire to be like her mother, she went to study literature in the Seminar ha-Kibbutzim in order "to enter this Parnassus" and to "sit at [her] mother's feet and have [her] mother caress [her] head" (pp. 123, 142). Avivit sees Gavriella as depicting herself in her "autobiographical novel" as "a Greek woman who has not converted to Judaism," like the wife of the famous poet Tchernichovsky's, a Greek woman who did not convert (p. 219). There are numerous erotic allusions. In a new hotel Gavriella sees the statue of a winged cupid in the garden. (p. 221). Then on her third day in Paris she goes to see the unicorn (in the painting "the Lady and the Unicorn") in the Museon de Cluny. Together with a former colleague, Arik, whom she meets, she sees Jean Anouille's *Antigone* while recollecting reflections about the power of love from Sophocles' *Antigone* (p. 227). Arik recites lines from Gavriella/Nogah's poem "Artemis," that was included in her first book of poetry—a book named ... *Persephone Zokheret* (p. 228). Avivit writes that the last chapter of the fictional biography of Nogah (not included in the present novel) is entitled "Ma'avar Jabbok," the Biblical allusion to Jacob's encounter with the angel near the river Jabbok. This is merged in the protagonist's mind through a dream in which Nogah sees herself swimming and drowning and unable to recall her name between Scylla and Charybidis. This is reminiscent of the treacherous straits traversed by the Argonauts in Homer's *The Odyssey*. After her "metamorphosis," Gavriella's husband recalls that Gavriella was always searching, "like the Greeks for the Golden Fleece"; when they were first married she had spent a weekend in Tsefat with some "God searchers." (p. 196). There is even a touch of farcical (Yiddish) humor when Gavriella's husband alludes to Gavriella's Greek obsession on the occasion of her trip to the Greek island of Naxos in order to study. Her husband says, "some poet Archilochus ... Architochus (p. 90).

78. Ibid., p. 228.
79. Ibid., p. 229.
80. Ibid., p. 77.
81. Ibid., pp. 119–120. Avivit notes (p. 142) that in her mother's "autobiographical novel," she is "a Greek woman who has not become Jewish."
82. Megged, *Ha-Ḥayyim ha-Qeṣarim*, pp. 46–48.
83. Ibid., p. 229.
84. Megged, *Ha-Gamal ha-Me'ofef*, pp. 210–211. The professor-critic Elisheva Tal-Blumenfeld from Megged's *Ha-Ḥayyim ha-Qeṣarim* reappears in *Ha-Gamal ha-Me'ofef* (pp. 61–63) as an ambitious and two-faced critic of the narrator's novel.
85. Cf. the earlier, yet more Kurzweilesque, caricature of the critic Shimshon Yaaqov Rosenthal in Megged's *Maḥberot Evyatar*, p. 82, who writes a devastating critique of Yosef Richter.
86. See the chapter entitled "Ma'aseh Nora she-Er'a be-'Irenu" in Megged's *Ha-Gamal ha-Me'ofef*, pp. 186–196.
87. Megged, *'Avel* (Tel Aviv, 1996), p. 234.

88. Ibid., pp. 215–216.

89. Ibid., p. 233.

90. This is a pun on the famous expression "*o ḥavruta o mitutah*," appearing at the end of the story of Ḥoni ha-Meʻaggel in Taʻanit 83A. Cf. Richter's comment in Megged's *Maḥberot Evyatar*, p. 73: "To be an author is a curse, inasmuch as one is a permanent slave to one's craft."

91. See Megged, "Ben ha-Maḥsomim," *Davar* (March 5, 1982), p. 13. The Irishman was amazed that a civilian can scream at a soldier the way one woman does who wants to return south without her I. D. Megged drives him to a place on the way to Yammit where there is a nasty confrontation between the settlers and the army.

92. Ibid. Megged gives the example of James Joyce, who "hated Catholicism because in his heart of hearts he loved it, and he chose a Jewish hero, Bloom . . . . and the [Irish and Jewish] rhetoric and humor" are also similar.

93. On the "underground man," see V. Brombert, *In Praise of Antiheroes*, pp. 31–42.

94. Megged, *Maḥberot Evyatar*, p. 121.

95. Ibid., pp. 121–124.

96. *ʻAvel*, pp. 222–223.

97. Ibid., pp. 221–223.

98. Ibid., pp. 232–233.

99. Megged, *Persephone Zokheret*, p. 232.

100. Ibid., p. 234.

101. Ibid., p. 261. Cf. Megged's interview with an artist friend name Ariella (quite close to Gavriella) in "Ḥeshbon ha-Nefesh u-Meqorot ha-Koʼaḥ—Monolog bi-Shene Peraqim," *Davar* (September 10, 1980), p. 3 and (September 19, 1980), pp. 11, 18; *Davar*, pp. 178–191; and in *Ezor ha-Raʻash* (Tel Aviv, 1985), pp. 178–191. And cf. Avivit's remarks in a slightly different vein in Megged's *Persephone Zokheret*, p. 143, in what she writes to her friend Shuli: "I am not anti-religious, Shuli. I even have a certain longing for religious faith, when I see how everything is exposed ("*parutz*") to all the winds (influences), without any respect for tradition, without moral restraint . . . " Cf. also the remarks of Albert Giḥon in *Gaʻaguʻim le-Olga*, pp. 214–215.

102. Megged, *Persephone Zokheret*, p. 155.

103. Ibid., p. 74.

104. Ibid., pp. 74–75.

105. Ibid., pp. 70–77. On pp. 92–93 Avivit recalls the episode when her mother said she was going to Kfar Blum to read her poems in a "festival of Mediterranean music." She doesn't show up there when she is supposed to. Avivit searches for her. Gavriella had gone off touring with a musician from Tangiers

106. Gavriella's father says it was a *"Schauspiel,"* i.e., she was putting on an act. Ibid., p. 193.

107. Ibid., pp. 192–193.

108. The story "Michah Shtoq" is in Megged, *Maʻaseh Megunneh* (Tel Aviv, 1986), pp.107–165. Previously, nine of Megged's newspaper columns appeared under the title "Michah Shtoq" in *Davar* (November 6, 13, 20, 27 and December 4, 1981 and January 8, 29, and February 5, 1982).

109. Megged, *Ha-Gamal ha-Me'ofef*, pp. 223-235

110. Supra, n. 22 and many similar expressions of Megged's proclivities, particularly in interviews following the publication of his various works.

111. Megged, *Foigelman*, p. 35. And see Adelbert von Chamisso, "The Strange Story of Peter Schlemihl" in *German Romantic Stories*, edited by Frank G. Ryder (New York, 1988), pp. 91-137.

112. Ernst Simon in the subsection of a lengthy article, entitled "Ha-Ish ha-Tov ve-he-Ḥalash ba-Sifrut ha-'Ivrit ha-Ḥadashah," *Sefer A. M. Dushkin* (Jerusalem, 1962), p. 282 and in English translation in *An Anthology of Hebrew Essays*, edited by Israel Cohen and B.Y. Michali, Vol. II, p. 329. According to Jennifer Speake, *The Oxford Dictionary of Foreign Words and Phrases* (New York, 1997), p. 384, "the word may ultimately be connected with the biblical Shelumiel, head of the tribe of Simeon (Numbers 1:6), who, according to the Talmud, came to an unfortunate end. Modern use of *schlemiel* is influenced by Adelbert von Chamisso's famous tale *Peter Schlemihls wundersame Geschichte* (1814), the eponymous hero of which sells his shadow."

113. Megged, *Foigelman*, p. 48.

114. Ibid.

115. See Megged's article "Reshimot mitaḥat la-Qav," *La-Merḥav* (November 30, 1956), p. 2 and the section of *Miqreh ha-Kesil* entitled "Ha-'Ir ha-Levanah."

116. Megged, *Miqreh ha-Kesil*, pp. 225-276 and see E. Simon, *Sefer A. M. Dushkin*, p. 285.

117. This explains the dismay of certain liberal intellectuals at what they perceived as Megged's increasing disaffection from the more pacifist stance that he was assumed to have formerly represented. See, for example, Ilana Hammerman, "Teshuvah le-Megged: Meqomekha ba-Ṣad Shellanu!" *Ha-Aretz* (November 22, 1988).

118. E. Simon, *Sefer A. M. Dushkin*, p. 284.

119. See Megged, *Miqreh ha-Kesil* p. 275 and the quotation of this remark by E. Simon, *Sefer A. M. Dushkin*, p. 284.

120. See Megged's interview with Nurit, "Ha-Paḥad ve-ha-Bushah ve-ha-Qiyyum ha-Yehudi," in *Orim la-Horim* (March, 1973). In 1937 at age 16, Megged was on a trip to Trumpeldor's shrine at Tel Hai in the Galil. It was the period of the Arab riots, and there was much tension. Near Tiberias a group of young Arab toughs threw stones at the bus. After arriving at the bus station the Jewish passengers rushed into a nearby restaurant. There they huddled against the walls while outside the *shabab* were wailing, and the sound of rocks could be heard. Suddenly, Megged sensed the same commingling of shame and terror. He recalled "the bitter taste of Jewish existence in the *galut*, which had suddenly invaded Eretz Yisra'el as well."

121. Ibid.

122. Megged, *Maḥberot Evyatar*, pp. 60, 65 et passim.

123. Megged, *Foigelman*, pp. 101-102.

124. V. Brombert, *In Praise of Antiheroes*, p. 66.

125. Ibid., pp. 66-67.

126. It is from one of Ya'aqov Levinstein's letters in Megged, *'Avel*, p. 219.

127. Albert Giḥon writes this in one of the letters that he writes to himself under the guise of Olga in *Ga'agu'im le-Olga*, p. 223.

Yoel Finkelman

HAREDI ISOLATION IN CHANGING ENVIRONMENTS: A CASE STUDY IN YESHIVA IMMIGRATION

> In this generation ... following the destruction in Europe, when the Torah centers were destroyed ... the lofty task of rebuilding the ruins falls on the Jews of America and the Land of Israel ... They must create an atmosphere of dedication to the Torah ... without involvement in any external and tangential things.[1]
> —Rabbi Aharon Kotler (c. 1943)

Haredi Judaism works hard to isolate itself from the non-Haredi elements in modern environments. Indeed, Haredi Judaism may be accurately defined by social and intellectual isolationism combined with strict adherence to halakhah, Jewish law. Obviously, this isolationism is not an all-or-nothing affair. Haredi communities are isolated from their cultural contexts to greater or less degrees, depending on how well they succeed in creating a social environment free from the outside influences they consider dangerous.[2] Both ideological as well as social factors affect the extent to which a given Haredi sub-culture finds extreme isolation both desirable and feasible. Haredi sub-communities develop in different cultural contexts. Hungary of the mid-nineteenth century, where Haredi Jewry first concretized its ultra-conservative ideology, differs significantly from the United States in the middle of the twentieth century, where many Haredi refugees fled from the Holocaust, which differs significantly from Meah She'arim or Bnei Brak in the independent State of Israel. In each context Haredi Jews may see the environment as threatening to a greater or lesser extent; they may see greater or lesser value in influencing "wrongdoers" outside their narrow community; they may be more or less successful at developing a social and economic infrastructure which allows for isolation. To more fully understand the social and religious history of Haredi Jewry, we must identify the ways in which differences in social and cultural contexts affect the contact which Haredi Jews have with non-Haredi people and ideas.

This essay will examine two yeshivas, both led by the staunchly Haredi R. Aharon Kotler, and the ways that social and ideological factors influence the relationship between the yeshiva and the given Jewish social environment.[3] Despite obvious similarities between the two institutions, they isolated themselves from their environments in different ways. This reflects crucial structural differences between Jewish society in Kletzk, Poland and that of the United States. We shall see that as the yeshiva moved from the relatively integrated and more organically Jewish towns of Eastern Europe to the more pluralistic and less traditional atmosphere in the United States, it tended toward greater isolation.

R. Kotler was the rosh yeshiva of two major yeshivas, 'Etz Hayyim in Kletzk, Poland and Beth Medrash Govoha [sic] in Lakewood, New Jersey. Both yeshivas followed the model of R. Hayyim Volozhin's Lithuanian yeshiva, originally founded in 1803. At that early date, R. Hayyim could not have predicted the severity of the religious and social crisis that would plague traditional Judaism later in the century.[4] He did not know, nor could he have known, that Haskalah, Zionism, socialism, and the modern social changes that helped support these ideologies would gradually push the majority of Eastern European Jews away from traditional halakhic behavior. In this changing environment the Lithuanian yeshiva became a most effective tool in the Orthodox battle against what it perceives as the corrupting influences of modernity. The yeshiva socializes teenage students into a powerful Orthodox atmosphere, and during this critical stage in the development of personal identity and sense of self, seeks to isolate them from the perceived dangers of the outside. It inculcates Orthodox attitudes and patterns of behavior, which many students take with them when they leave, and which they may then pass along to their own children and students. The yeshiva education grants students competence in the vast and highly complex world of Talmud and Rabbinic literature, while depriving them of systematic general or vocational education that might help them succeed outside of a rabbinical profession. Yeshiva graduates are likely to be Orthodox, and remain Orthodox their entire lives.

In 1897 Rabbi Ya'akov David Willowsky of Slutzk (Ridvaz), a small town located on the Russian side of the Russian-Polish border, hoped to improve the spiritual and religious atmosphere in his community, which he felt had been damaged by the forces of modernization and Haskalah. He turned to R. Natan Tzvi Finkel, famed spiritual leader of the yeshiva in Slobodka, asking him to send a handful of students to begin a yeshiva. Yeshivat 'Etz Hayyim was born when fourteen young men arrived in Slutzk, under the leadership of R. Isser Zalman Meltzer, who served as rosh yeshiva and later as the town's rabbi after R. Willowsky left Europe.[5] In 1914 R. Meltzer's daughter was married to one of the leading students in the Slobodka yeshiva, the twenty-two-year-old R. Aharon Kotler. R. Kotler moved to Slutzk, and became an integral part of the yeshiva staff.

Over the course of the next decade, R. Kotler became a more influential force in the yeshiva. At first, he took on a few teaching and administrative responsibilities. With the Russian Revolution in 1917, and a developing Soviet policy of persecuting yeshivas, R. Meltzer found himself and the yeshiva under careful surveillance, and he was briefly jailed a few times. During R. Meltzer's absences, R. Kotler took on more responsibilities. In 1921, the persecution became so severe that the yeshiva chose to split into two groups. The first group, under the leadership of R. Kotler, fled across the border to Kletzk, Poland, safe from Soviet persecution.[6] Kletzk Jewry accepted the yeshiva students warmly, allowing them to use the main synagogue as a study hall. The second group, under R. Meltzer's leadership, remained in Slutzk so that R. Meltzer could continue his work as communal rabbi. Soviet persecution, however, intensified, forcing more students to escape to the safer Kletzk, until R. Meltzer himself finally made the trip in 1923. When R. Meltzer left for Palestine in 1924, R. Kotler found himself in the position of sole rosh yeshiva.

The transition in leadership pushed the yeshiva in a more Haredi direction. R. Meltzer was considerably more moderate than his son-in-law in reference to Zionism, general education, and isolation from the prevalent population of non-yeshiva Jews. R. Meltzer had been born a generation earlier than his son-in-law, in a less stormy and more traditional Eastern European Jewish atmosphere. He had fostered Zionist inclinations since his youth, and had even been a member of Nes Tziyonah, the underground Zionist organization of the yeshiva in Volozhin. He was generally a moderate voice as a member of the Mo'etzet Gedolei HaTorah, the governing body of the Orthodox Agudat Yisrael political party. Further, his choice to take on the responsibilities of communal rabbi in Slutzk stemmed from his concern for the uneducated, common Jew, a concern that R. Kotler did not share to nearly the same degree.[7] R. Meltzer even supported a Slutzk school which actively pursued general education along with the Torah curriculum.[8] R. Kotler was far more radical in his rejection of Zionism, in his isolationist approach to yeshiva life, and in his attitude toward the dangers of non-yeshiva influences. Some measure of tension developed between the two figures over these issues, which is exemplified by a particularly revealing incident that occurred during R. Meltzer's short stay in Kletzk in 1924. When R. Kotler heard that one of his students, Moshe Chigier, wanted to emigrate to Palestine in order to study with the more Zionist and intellectually open R. Avraham Isaac Kook, R. Kotler unceremoniously expelled him from the yeshiva. Chigier approached R. Meltzer with his crisis, and the rabbi took the student into his own home, providing him with room and board, while assisting him with the preparations for travel, and helping him gain the necessary visas.[9] When I asked Chigier how R. Meltzer could disregard the rosh yeshiva's orders, he indicated that the tension between the two was not new. It seems likely that this tension contributed to R. Meltzer's decision to leave for Palestine. It may even help explain why the yeshiva split into two groups, rather than remaining unified, and certainly influenced the choice that students had to make between remaining in Slutzk or leaving for Kletzk. Whatever the yeshivas internal politics, R. Kotler's growing role in yeshiva life pushed the institution toward greater social and intellectual isolation.

During the 1920s and 1930s the reputation of both the yeshiva and R. Kotler grew, as more students flocked to the yeshiva and as R. Kotler became more active and influential in Agudat Yisrael politics. In 1929, when the yeshiva grew so big that it could no longer fit into the synagogue, it dedicated its own building in the center of town. The outbreak of World War II, however, brought this period of growth to a tragic close. Like so many other yeshivas at the time, it quickly fled to Vilna, which had just been transferred to the still independent and neutral Lithuania, but it did not stay there long. Fearful of the effect that big city life might have on his students, the yeshiva split into three groups, each group making its way to a smaller outlying town. When the Soviet Union occupied Lithuania later in 1939 and annexed it in 1940, the yeshiva simply collapsed.

R. Kotler escaped Europe at the last possible moment, finding temporary refuge in Japan before arriving permanently in the United States in 1941. Immediately upon his arrival, he dedicated himself to the physical salvation of European Jewry, throwing himself wholeheartedly into the Va'ad Hatzalah, an Orthodox organization active in the rescue effort.[10] In 1942 a small informal group of yeshiva students from White Plains, a suburb of New York City, asked R. Kotler to serve as their teacher and rosh yeshiva. Reluctant to cease his work with Va'ad Hatzalah, but always eager to teach Torah, R. Kotler agreed under three conditions. First, the students would move further from New York City. Second, initially R. Kotler would study with the students only on weekends, freeing the rest of his week for rescue work. Finally, he would be the sole authority on educational and policy decisions. A short time later, in 1943, Beth Medrash Govoha opened its doors in the small resort town of Lakewood, New Jersey. Beginning with only fourteen mostly European students, it grew quickly, attracting quite a few European refugees together with a growing number of American-born youth. By the time of R. Kotler's death in 1962, the yeshiva had grown to be one of America's largest Lithuanian-style yeshivas. Some

200 single and married students, most of them American born, studied there, and a group of teachers and students had already been sent to Philadelphia to begin a branch there. Today, Beth Medrash Govoha is known as one of the world's largest yeshivas, boasting some 1300 students.[11]

Throughout his long career, R. Kotler staunchly supported the Agudat Yisrael political party, becoming a member and later head of its governing body, the Mo'etzet Gedolei HaTorah. Perhaps more so than other Agudists, he vigorously opposed Zionism, socialism, Haskalah, as well as other ideologies that developed among Eastern European Jewry. In America, he insisted that Orthodoxy refuse contact with the non-Orthodox denominations. He urged his students to avoid general education of any kind, and would not allow any students in Lakewood to attend college. It is not at all surprising that Lakewood was the most extremely isolationist of the Lithuanian-style yeshivas in America.

Both yeshivas, Kletzk and Lakewood, followed the Lithuanian tradition. The students in their teens and twenties studied Talmud almost exclusively, although some time was set aside each day for *musar*, ethical self-development. Both yeshivas opposed student involvement in other concerns, particularly general education, Zionism, or other professions. Although many students from both yeshivas later went on to careers in Jewish education or the rabbinate, the yeshiva was not designed to train rabbis or educators, but Torah scholars. Both yeshivas, in fact, saw themselves as bastions of Orthodoxy in an increasingly hostile environment. Both yeshivas succeeded in training many highly motivated and dedicated alumni who viewed Torah study as the Jew's ultimate goal, and non-Torah pursuits as sinful. Yet, despite these similarities, there were subtle differences in their relationship to the threatening environments, which in large part can be traced to the differences between interwar Poland and post-war America. The differences between the two yeshivas indicate R. Kotler's growing rejection of the non-Haredi trends in Jewish life. Ironically, however, they also demonstrate the marked advantages that America's secular democracy held for his yeshiva and its developing isolationist agenda.

'Etz Hayyim, home to a few hundred neatly dressed, clean-shaven[12] students, was located within a small, almost entirely Jewish community. The town of Kletzk housed some 4000 people, nearly three quarters of whom were Jews. Inevitably, the yeshiva was part and parcel of town life. Overall, Kletzk was a more traditional town than other interwar Jewish towns. Still, the town's residents and their beliefs hardly met with R. Kotler's approval. The majority of Kletzk townspeople did not identify with R. Kotler, the yeshiva, or the Haredi Agudat Yisrael political party. Even local Orthodox Jews identified more with the Zionist groups than with Agudah. Others identified with the non-Orthodox

Zionist movements, the Haskalah-oriented Tarbut school, socialist organizations, and the like which developed in Kletzk while the yeshiva was there. The town housed numerous influences that might be considered dangerous to a yeshiva student.[13]

The students, however, could hardly avoid contact with these influences, as they came in daily contact with the community's goings on. When the yeshiva first moved to Kletzk it was housed in the center of town, within the community's largest synagogue. The new separate building, which was completed in 1929, was also located in the heart of the town. Students lived in the homes of local homeowners and ate at their tables, paying for room and board from a yeshiva stipend, all standard practice in Lithuanian yeshivas at the time.[14] Most of these homeowners—who did not fully identify with the yeshiva, with R. Kotler, or with Agudat Yisrael—accepted boarders primarily for economic reasons, rather than ideological ones. According to some reports, a few yeshiva students even lived in the homes of non-Orthodox Jews. Students could not help but speak to the homeowners with whom they boarded, and perhaps even be influenced by their ideas. Even the yeshiva's new building did not include a dormitory, which might have helped isolate students from townspeople. Dormitories were not yet common in Eastern European yeshivas, Yeshivat Hakhmei Lublin being the rare exception. Even had R. Kotler preferred isolating students from the community by housing them separately, a dormitory would require a greater financial and administrative effort than the yeshiva could reasonably afford.

Despite potential tensions, the yeshiva and its students lived on fairly good terms with at least the majority of the town's Jews. A few students were involved enough in local life to meet, socialize with, and marry local young women, despite R. Kotler's dissatisfaction, and one former student joked that socializing with girls from town was an occasional forbidden pastime for the most daring students. The yeshiva invited local Jews to the *Simhat Torah* and *Purim* celebrations, although there is no indication of how many actually attended. As Y. Epstein, a former student put it, "The yeshiva students urbanized [*sic*] into Kletzk, and enjoyed a fatherly relationship with the city's population."[15] Although he could be accused of oversimplification or forgetfulness, particularly in the context of a memorial volume, other students support his claim. A few recalled greater tension between the yeshiva and townspeople in other towns in which they studied, but little such tension in Kletzk.[16]

Even had R. Kotler preferred to move the yeshiva geographically outside the influence of the increasingly non-Orthodox Jewish community, a number of factors prevented him from doing so. First and foremost, Polish Jews were partially governed by the kehillah, an elected semi-autonomous religio-political body. Jews were members of the kehillah by Polish law, and could not create independent religious communities.[17] R. Kotler later indicated that he prefers separate Orthodox communities when possible, but that that was impossible in Poland.[18] Moving to the larger cities, where the yeshiva might maintain greater anonymity, would hardly have helped, as cities were less religious and more subject to distractions and non-Orthodox ideologies than the smaller towns. In fact, when the yeshiva was forced into Vilna at the beginning of the World War II, R. Kotler quickly left, fearing the city's numerous distractions. Similarly, the yeshiva could not attempt to establish itself outside the Jewish communities. Latent and not-so-latent anti-Semitism among Polish gentiles would not tolerate a yeshiva of Orthodox Jews in their midst. Furthermore, many Russian students stayed in Poland illegally, and the yeshiva could do nothing to call attention to itself.

In short, the yeshiva and the community maintained relations of mutual dependence. The yeshiva relied on the community for housing, food, and a safe Jewish environment. The yeshiva students' housing and food provided the community with an important source of income, money that the yeshiva had raised outside the community.[19] The yeshiva may also have provided the townspeople, or at least its Orthodox residents, with a sense of pride and respect relative to other towns without such a prestigious yeshiva. Self-interest pushed both sides to help maintain peaceful and integrated relations.[20]

Furthermore, there were good ideological and religious reasons for involvement in the community. The yeshiva wanted to have some influence on Kletzk Jews. Like other outgrowths of Slobodka, the yeshiva was originally brought to Slutzk to help strengthen Orthodoxy within a community increasingly sympathetic to non-Orthodox trends. It took this goal seriously, establishing an elementary school to help bring its message to Kletzk youth.[21] R. Kotler also served as a leading member of the Kletzk kehillah.[22] Like the Agudat Yisrael political party he represented, R. Kotler strove to restore Orthodox hegemony over Jewish public issues. The kehillah system was a central battleground in the debates between Zionists, Agudists, socialists, assimilationists, and others over creating and forming Jewish cultural, national, and religious identity in the reconstructed Poland. National debates between these different ideologies were translated to the communal level in the kehillah, and R. Kotler could not allow his Orthodox position to go unheard. Furthermore, Agudat Yisrael believed that it represented the silent majority of Polish Jews. From Agudah's perspective, the average working man, the Polish Jewish shopkeeper or craftsman, remained dedicated to *mitzvot*, Torah study, Orthodoxy, and a traditional lifestyle. Consequently, R. Kotler and the Agudah within the kehillah were still fighting for hegemony and complete control over Jewish concerns. They hoped, and probably expected, to simply win the fight against Zionism, Haskalah, and religious indifference.[23] Beyond that, the yeshiva required representation in the kehillah to secure the community's ongoing financial and political support. For example, R. Kotler lobbied hard to gain the support necessary to build the yeshiva's new building, and was active in garnering support for other Orthodox concerns, like the Beit Ya'akov school.[24] It seems that R. Kotler hoped to keep his students out of political organizations, but he could hardly shield them from local and national Jewish politics.

We do not know if R. Kotler would have preferred a more isolated yeshiva in Europe. However, years of inertia would make it difficult to implement such a policy. Lithuanian yeshivas had always been at least somewhat integrated with local communities. The move from Slutzk to Kletzk might have created an opportunity to rewrite some of the social ground rules. But, the yeshiva had fled Russia in the middle of the night, and the yeshiva students lacked the most basic necessities: food, housing, and a place to study. At the time, the yeshiva quite desperately needed the good will of Kletzk Jewry.

These limits on yeshiva isolation notwithstanding, R. Kotler preferred the Eastern European shtetl to any other alternative, and opposed any attempt by yeshiva students to leave Europe, at least until the end of 1939. As imperfect as things were, the alternatives were far worse from his perspective. America, of course, was the *treyfe medineh*, and held little apparent promise for Orthodox yeshiva students, or so he thought before he himself came there. We have already seen how radically he opposed Chigier's desire to move to a yeshiva in Palestine. R. Kotler viewed Palestine as a free and irreligious atmosphere which lacked an adequate yeshiva infrastructure to protect European students.[25] As late as 1939, R. Kotler referred to immigration certificates as "toilet paper."[26]

When R. Kotler moved to America, however, he discovered a social, ideological, and financial context that allowed for a great deal more isolation than he had achieved in Europe. He had a wonderful opportunity to start anew, to create a yeshiva as isolated from American Jewry as conditions would allow. Few of the aforementioned obstacles to isolation existed in America. Separation of religion from state meant that the American government could not recognize Jews as an independent social or legal entity, as the Polish government had. Consequently, the yeshiva was not bound to a kehillah, or any other public body with any formal authority. It was free to go it alone.

Small, primarily Jewish towns like Kletzk did not exist in America, so R. Kotler's choices for the yeshiva's location were limited. The Jewish neighborhoods in New York came with all the distractions of the big city. Since smaller, primarily gentile, towns would contain fewer distractions, R. Kotler chose to move the yeshiva outside of New York to the small resort town of Lakewood, New Jersey. Indeed, he only agreed to become rosh yeshiva of the White Plains study group on condition that they moved away from New York. Lakewood was about an hour's drive from New York, close enough to attract students, yet far enough to isolate them from New York and the larger community. Furthermore, R. Kotler hoped he could convince the wealthy Jews who vacationed in Lakewood to support the yeshiva financially. The Christian majority in Lakewood would naturally be socially distant from the Orthodox yeshiva students, and the small Jewish minority could be ignored with relative ease.[27] The American tradition of religious tolerance and the relative lack of violent anti-Semitism allowed R. Kotler the luxury of establishing a large Jewish institution in a predominantly gentile area.

Furthermore, R. Kotler had little motivation to remain in New York, the home of a well-established Jewish community which R. Kotler viewed as almost entirely degenerate. The majority of identifying American Jews associated with the Reform and Conservative movements—the "forgeries of Torah," as R. Kolter referred to them[28]—which were both growing rapidly in America's religious revival of the 1950s. In addition, America's non-haredi Orthodox community was "happily Americanizing" for the most part. Interwar Orthodoxy was characterized by its inconsistent halakhic observance, rapid acculturation into American society, and lack of grass-roots ideological commitment.[29] R. Kotler accused "'Modern Orthodoxy' of introducing a small measure of modernization and small 'insignificant' changes. [In fact], this is the principle of Reform, and is the heart of the flight from Torah and fear [of God] in recent generations." He blasts those Orthodox Jews who cooperate with the Reform and Conservative movements, declaring that this is the equivalent of "denying the entire Torah, even that part which [they still] maintain." R. Kotler calls leaders of this community, "Haters of God, who do not desire the performance of His service." R. Kotler was more supportive of and more accepted in the community of New York yeshivas, but at times he even had very harsh things to say about their minor compromises with American reality and their acquiescence to college education. "There are some good people who still follow the path of minor compromises, on the assumption that they are choosing the least possible evil. This is a serious and bitter error. In the end, through their path of compromise, they will arrive at the greater evil. . . . May God enlighten their eyes."[30]

In this American context, R. Kotler could leave New York wholeheartedly, realizing that he could have little influence over New York Jewry. There was no illusion that a Haredi approach would defeat, or even have significant influence over, the secure non-Haredi denominations, at least in the immediate future. By the time R. Kotler arrived, the average American Jew had already chosen a path much different than R. Kotler's. There was no silent majority of "Torah-true" constituents to defend. In Poland, where there was a perceived hope of gaining a controlling influence over the community, the effort to do so was worth the price paid in social contact with dangerous trends. When Haredi Jewry was weak and defensive, as it was in post-war America, the price for involvement and influence was too high to pay. Naturally, the yeshiva turned inward. R. Kotler simply wrote off the "deviant" denominations as a lost cause, at least in the short term, and urged his students to do likewise.

Furthermore, once in Lakewood there was little reason to be involved in local political concerns. Lakewood was a gentile town,[31] and there was no kehillah or communal organ through which R. Kotler might wield any influence over Lakewood's Jewish minority. In America R. Kotler focused his political activism on the national and international level, rather than the local city level, as he had in Poland. The Agudat Yisrael organization on a national level, and more importantly in Israel, remained crucial to the Jewish future. Lakewood city politics only mattered in an instrumental way, when the yeshiva required building permits or the like, issues that were much less ideologically loaded than the makeup of the shtetl's kehillah. This helped distance political distractions from the four walls of the study hall.

The American context also made it that much more critical to protect the yeshiva student from the existing community. In Poland, a former yeshiva student could open a shop or work as a craftsman while avoiding direct contact with general education and the gentile world. He could remain in the shtetl, getting some limited vocational training from Jews, with whom he would later do business. He could remain in the relatively integrated Jewish community with a more traditional, even if imperfect, religious atmosphere. A student from Lakewood did not have that luxury. Once he left yeshiva, he would be cast directly into America's catastrophic religious environment. Professional training in America meant secular college, and even an uneducated shopkeeper would have more contact with America's non-Jewish world, and the thoroughly inadequate Jewish culture, than his Polish shtetl counterpart. In this context, leaving yeshiva must have been seen as much more threatening, and it became more important to protect the student from it.

Thus, the students in Lakewood lived in a dormitory and ate in a central dining hall. R. Kotler built the dormitory for both educational and pragmatic reasons. A dormitory has a profound impact on the educational institution's ability to mold the complete character of the student. When living in a dormitory, the student would leave the confines of the yeshiva only rarely, and the yeshiva administration could keep almost constant watch over his activities. Twenty-four hours a day, the institution and its goals mold the student's environment and identity. When a student transgresses the written and unwritten rules, a response is quick in coming. Less so when he lives in the room of his choice. Hence, the yeshiva administration had less control over the student's leisure time in Kletzk than in Lakewood. In Lakewood, R. Kotler could more actively prevent contact between students and the larger Jewish community. Lakewood students were permitted to return to New York and their parents only very rarely, limiting the influence that New York Jewry might have on them. The yeshiva also successfully limited student daily contact with local Lakewood residents, Jews or gentiles.[32] The yeshiva in Lakewood came much closer to what Erving Goffman calls a "total institution," one in which "a large number of like-situated individuals, cut off from the wider society and for an appreciable period of time, together lead an enclosed, formally administered round life."[33]

The dormitory and dining hall also made an important contribution to the yeshiva's recruitment. Many Lakewood students grew up in the New York Orthodox community, which R. Kotler had so sharply criticized. Their parents had provided their sons with Orthodox education through high school, even hoping they would study in the yeshiva for a short while before attending college and entering the workplace. But they saw Beth Medrash Govoha and R. Kotler's ideology as far too extreme. The New York yeshivas understood that many students would eventually leave the yeshiva, finding employment outside its walls. To facilitate this they allowed students to attend college while studying in yeshiva. Students in Beth Medrash Govoha were prohibited from acquiring any college education, and R. Kotler urged his students not to attend college even were they to leave yeshiva. Furthermore, R. Kotler publicly urged all of his students to remain in yeshiva indefinitely, although he was aware that many would leave, and he quietly urged some to work as teachers or community rabbis.[34] Many parents strongly preferred the New York yeshivas to R. Kotler's no-college alternative, and they often opposed their sons' choice to study in Lakewood.[35] The dormitory and dining hall, as well as stipends for married students, changed the dynamics of arguments between parents and children over if and where to attend yeshiva. The fact that the child does not require the parent's financial assistance to attend Beth Medrash Govoha gives him important leverage in influencing his parents to accept his choice, and allows him the freedom to ignore his parents' concerns should they refuse to see things his way.

R. Kotler paid a price for the dormitory, as it required considerable financial and administrative outlay. Once he decided to move from New

York, however, he had no choice but to build a dormitory. Outside major Jewish communities he would be hard-pressed to find enough kosher homes with extra rooms for rent. Furthermore, America was considerably wealthier than Kletzk, and homeowners were less pressed to take boarders. Also, the wealthy American Jewish community could more easily provide adequate funds for building and maintaining a dormitory.

But raising money is never an easy task, and one would suspect that isolationism and rejection of the larger community's values would make this task still more difficult. In some sense, however, the opposite was true. In the post-Holocaust years some American Jewish philanthropists felt nostalgia for the destroyed Jewish communities, which represented the heritage of the past. The uncompromising, isolationist, Yiddish-speaking, bearded rabbi on a self-declared crusade to transplant the European yeshiva to American soil could play on that nostalgic longing for authenticity and antiquity for which some Americans were looking. Indeed, many of the yeshiva's donors did not identify with Orthodoxy, let alone the yeshiva, in terms of ideology, personal commitment, or lifestyle.[36] Initially, the White Plains group guaranteed that R. Kotler would have no financial responsibilities,[37] but R. Kotler came to understand that the force of his vision and personality were necessary for effective fundraising. Orthodox activists set up personal and public meetings between R. Kotler and both Orthodox and non-Orthodox philanthropists. R. Kotler did not hide his views from potential donors. He subtly criticized Orthodox businessmen for their very involvement in making money, rather than learning Torah. He did not hide the differences between his own vision and that of contemporary American Jewry. According to some stories, he even berated non-Orthodox philanthropists to their faces.[38] This odd fundraising method worked, in part, due to R. Kotler's refusal to compromise his Eastern European Orthodox values, which impressed some donors and played on post-Holocaust nostalgia.

R. Kotler managed to develop social and intellectual isolation in Lakewood without economic self-sufficiency, which made his yeshiva different than other American isolationist religious groups. Certain Mennonite groups created isolated agricultural communities, where economic self-sufficiency reinforced social isolation. These groups prided themselves on an integrated communal life, founded on separate social institutions, which all but eliminated contact between group members and the larger society. To a lesser degree, the urban Hasidic communities of Brooklyn reinforced social isolation by earning their own living. Working-class adherents, who often worked in Hasidic owned businesses, imbibed Hasidic values in their daily working lives, and used their money to help support the community's socio-religious infrastructure.[39] In Lakewood, R. Kotler had no interest in anything but Torah study, which he viewed as the only important human endeavor. Gentiles could wash the floor, grow the food, and clean the streets as long as enough outside donations were collected to pay them for their efforts and to free the yeshiva students for Torah study. This was not a closed, self-sufficient society, but an isolated institution within a larger cultural environment that provided the yeshiva with its material and financial needs.[40]

In the American context, R. Kotler was ideologically, financially, and politically free to set out on his own. Beth Medrash Govoha and the larger American Jewish community did not depend on each other. The yeshiva did not need housing or food from the local community. It needed only funding, which it could gain by appeal to a relatively small, but distant, group of individuals. No individual Jewish communal organization had enough formal authority to make the yeshiva dependent on it. The American Jewish community did not need the yeshiva at all. R. Kotler would preach to his students that full-time Torah study is the Jew's lifeblood, that the community needed yeshiva students,[41] but the community itself would hardly have agreed with that sentiment. Nobody on either side had a strong interest in creating close social relations.

In both yeshivas, of course, some students were distracted by outside influences, as complete social isolation is not realistic. Lithuanian yeshivas have combated student interest in general education for as long as Haskalah influenced Eastern European Jews. Still, European yeshivas were notoriously permeable to outside literature and ideas, and Kletzk was no exception.[42] Some former students reported that neither they nor any other students had time or inclination for non-yeshiva concerns. Other reports differ. At least one Slutzk student speaks of reading Haskalah literature in the outhouse of the yeshiva before he eventually left for university.[43] Chigier would frequent the local library, and would even sneak away from the yeshiva to study with a teenage girl who would tutor him in mathematics and Russian.[44] They were certainly not the only examples. According to some reports, R. Kotler's own sister, who later became a prominent mathematician, attempted to persuade R. Kotler to leave the yeshiva for the university when he was young.[45]

Some students disagreed more openly with the isolationist and Agudist goals which the yeshiva administration and R. Kotler advocated. Yitzhak Halevi Epstein, both a local resident and student of the yeshiva, speaks of his warm relationship to the yeshiva and to R. Kotler in particular. He does not consider it odd that he and his family were ardent Zionists who acquired general education.[46] Other Mizrahi-inclined students did not feel that they were treated quite as well, and they turned to Zerah Warhaftig, the Religious-Zionist activist and later the Israeli Minister of Religion, to help them confront the yeshiva's administration.[47] Before moving to Palestine, Chigier was influenced by the local Zionist youth who prepared to emigrate to Palestine, by the Zionist press, and by the more open and worldly approach of R. Abraham Isaac Kook. R. Isser Zalman Meltzer's Zionist views certainly influenced those students who knew him or recalled the period of his involvement in the yeshiva. It seems that some students were at least somewhat active in Zionist or Agudat Yisrael politics, which R. Kotler opposed, but could do little about.[48]

Unfortunately, the available data is spotty and anecdotal making it impossible to generalize about the extent of this kind of activity. Distractions, however, certainly existed, and some students took advantage of them, either on the sly or out in the open. Since the yeshiva was so integrated with the larger community, however, it was still able to attract students who did not see eye to eye, religiously or ideologically, with R. Kotler or the institution's administration.

Lakewood, however, was less likely to attract students with an immediate desire for a college education or with strong Zionist leanings. One would suspect that outside interests would be more available to American students. The American Jewish community was less traditional and better educated than the Kletzk community. Almost all American students would have completed a minimal high school education before arriving in Lakewood, making them more worldly and educated than their average Polish counterpart. An American Lakewood student had to reject the general education he already possessed, while the Kletzk student needed only to be shielded from something with which he had had very little contact in the past. Some students speculated that the social distance between European-educated and American-educated students in Lakewood stemmed from the formers' greater expertise in the Talmud, and their limited general education. No doubt, many Lakewood students eventually attended university after leaving the yeshiva, and many later pursued secular careers.[49] Others probably became interested in Zionism or other non-Torah issues before, during, or after their stay in Lakewood. Again, we lack adequate data to measure this precisely.

Despite this, students with a more immediate drive to a college education could very easily attend one of the New York yeshivas. Similarly, Zionist students would feel less inclined to go to Lakewood, where they would be effectively isolated from other Zionist activists. Not surprisingly, Lakewood gained a reputation as a place of more serious and intense learning than the New York yeshivas.[50] That is to say, Lakewood's isolationist stance created a process of student self-selection, in which only the most dedicated and serious students would choose to attend. As one early Lakewood student put it, "If you want to be a *bahur* (unmarried yeshiva student) from Lakewood, you had to be *masur* (dedicated) to Torah 100%.... Chaim Berlin and Torah VaDa'as were good yeshivas, but the *bahurim* went there to college at night sometimes.... If you want a place where you could 100% be *masur* to *limmud haTorah* (Torah study) and *yiras Shamayim* (fear of Heaven) [you went to Lakewood]." Obviously, ideological identification with R. Kotler's isolationist, Torah-only, concerns were not the only factors to help student recruitment. Some students may have been attracted to R. Kotler's personality or study method. Others, in an act of young-adult rebellion, may have wanted to distance themselves geographically from their parents, or from mainstream American values. Yet, this process of self-selection helped R. Kotler keep pernicious literature and influences out of the yeshiva's walls, in ways that were less effective in the more integrated context of Kletzk Jewish culture.

Before the founding of Beth Medrash Govoha, there had been numerous previous attempts to recreate Lithuanian-style yeshivas in the United States. Inevitably, these schools found it necessary—whether due to ideological commitment or sheer necessity—to accommodate themselves to certain American educational and cultural values. From Yeshiva 'Etz Hayyim's development into Yeshiva University, to Torah VaDa'as's relatively progressive educational approach, to the almost universal acceptance of the necessity of college education for some students, these schools found ways to make yeshivas more compatible with American Orthodoxy. In part, they did so by consciously training students for the American workplace, preparing them for careers as rabbis or teachers.[51] In contrast, R. Kotler found ways to use American cultural, social, and economic resources to further distance his yeshiva and its students from what he saw as an almost unmitigated American religious disaster. Yeshivas should not compromise with American values in the hope of attracting more students, and should make no conscious effort to prepare students for the job market, even for work as religious functionaries. Instead, they should attract the few uncompromising students still willing to flee from American Judaism to do nothing but study Torah.

Indeed, this was simply an extreme version of the overall spirit that began to gain greater influence in American Orthodoxy since World War II, a process that Jeffrey Gurock called "The Winnowing of American Orthodoxy."[52] The Orthodox community was becoming more ideological self-conscious and less willing to accept non-committed Jews into the community or its institutions. The phenomenon of the "Non-Observant Orthodox"—the Jews who flocked to Orthodox synagogues despite their personal lack of commitment to halakhic behavior[53]— gradually disappeared as the older generation died off. The next generation, supported by the influx of more committed refugees, developed an increasingly tight knit, more strongly exclusionist, and more halakhically committed community. R. Kotler, Beth Medrash Govoha, and the yeshiva's alumni were not only examples of these changes, but to this day are active leaders in helping to bring them about.

Ironically, it was the secular nature of American culture that claims much of the credit for Beth Medrash Govoha's success. The more Jewish and more traditional context of Eastern Europe made it more difficult for R. Kotler to create an environment of undistracted Torah study. The more secular, the more apparently pernicious American context, allowed him to isolate his students more thoroughly from all non-Torah concerns. The creation and development of this environment helped turn Beth Medrash Govoha into what it became after R. Kotler's death, the largest yeshiva in America.

THE HEBREW UNIVERSITY OF JERUSALEM

NOTES

I would like to thank all those who read and commented on drafts of this paper: my father, R. Dr. Eliezer Finkelman, Dr. Eli Lederhendler, Dr. Kimmy Caplan, and Prof. Aviezer Ravitzky. In particular, Dr. Shaul Stampfer's continual advice and helpful suggestions were exceedingly beneficial.

1. *Quntres Keter Torah*, pp. 31–32 (below, n. 3).

2. On the tension between isolation and the influence of the outside world in Haredi society, see Menachem Friedman, "Haredim Confront the Modern City," *Studies in Contemporary Jewry*, Vol. 2 (1986), pp. 74–96; Samuel C. Heilman and Menachem Friedman, "Religious Fundamentalism and Religious Jews: The Case of the Haredim," in *Fundamentalisms Observed*, edited by Martin E. Marty and R. Scott Appleby (Chicago, 1991), pp. 197–264; and Haym Soloveitchik, "Rupture and Reconstruction: The Transformation of Contemporary Orthodoxy," *Tradition*, Vol. 28, No. 4 (1994), pp. 64–128.

3. Unfortunately, the academic literature has not granted adequate attention to R. Kotler or Beth Medrash Govoha, despite their profound influence on American Haredi Jewry. The American Haredi community recognizes R. Kotler as one of its founders, crediting him—together with R. Shraga Feivel Mendelowitz and a few others—with bringing what it calls authentic Torah to America, at a time when almost nobody, even many Haredi leaders, thought it possible. By now, Lakewood is recognized as one of the world's largest yeshivas, and it expands its influence through a network of full time *kollel* programs scattered throughout North America. R. Kotler was a commanding force in Agudat Yisrael for decades, not to mention activism in other Haredi organizations like Va'ad Hatzalah, Torah UMessorah, and Hinnukh 'Atzma'i.

Despite the lack of academic literature, a number of Orthodox biographical sketches of R. Kotler exist, which must be used with requisite caution. Fishel

Galerentler and A. Avi-Shefer, *Maran HaGaon Rabbi Aharon Kotler Zt"l: Rabban Shel Kol Benei HaGolah* [Our Teacher Rabbi Aharon Kolter: The Rabbi of the Entire Exile] (New York, 1964). Alter Pekier, *Reb Aharon: An Appreciation of the Great Gaon, Tzaddik and Manhig HaDor* [Genius, Righteous One, and Leader of the Generation], *the Kletzk-Lakewood Rosh HaYeshivah, Moreinu HaRav Aharon Kotler* (New York, 1995). Pekier studied with R. Kotler both in Kletzk and in America. Aharon Sorsky, *Marbitzei Torah UMusar* [Disseminators of Torah and Ethics] (Brooklyn, 1977), Vol. 3, pp. 215-266 includes a lengthy biography, as well as a number of letters and primary sources. Marvin Schick, "*Rav Aharon Lo Meit*: The Legacy of Rav Aharon Kotler," *Jewish Action*, Vol. 48 (1988), pp. 77-85. Chaim Shapiro, "From Kletzk to Lakewood, U.S.A." in *The Torah World*, edited by Nissen Wolpin, (Brooklyn, 1982), pp. 184-205. Shaul Kagan, "Reb Aharon Kotler *zt"l*: Ten Years After His Passing," *The Jewish Observer*, Vol. 9, No. 3, pp. 3-13. Akiva Egozi was kind enough to send me a copy of his "*LeDemut Diyukno Shel HaGaon R. Aharon Kotler, zt"l*" [Toward and Image of the Personality of R. Aharon Kotler], which appeared in an unspecified volume of *Derakhim VaDerekh BeHinnukh*. Yediel Meltzer, *BeDerekh 'Etz Hayyim* [In the Path of 'Etz Hayyim] (Jerusalem, 1986), a collection of memoirs about R. Isser Zalman Meltzer, also contains information about R. Kotler. Amos Bunim's biography of his father, Irving M. Bunim, a longtime Orthodox activist and close friend of R. Kotler, includes numerous photographs and anecdotes throughout. See *A Fire in His Soul: Irving M. Bunim, 1901-1980: The Man and His Impact on American Orthodox Jewry*, (Jerusalem, 1989). Yonason Rosenblum reports a few incidents from R. Kotler's youth in his *Reb Yaakov: The Life and Times of HaGaon Rabbi Yaakov Kamenetsky*, (Brooklyn, 1993). Jacob J. Schachter refers to R. Kotler's opposition to R. Mendelowitz's attempt to open a private college for yeshiva students in the 1940s. See his "Facing the Truths of History," *The Torah U-Madda Journal*, Vol. 8 (1998-1999), pp. 200-276 (p. 223 in particular), and the works cited there. R. Zerah Warhaftig refers to his contact with R. Kotler throughout his book on his attempts to gain exit visas for yeshiva leaders and students during World War II, *Palit VeSarid BiYmei HaShoah* [Refugee and Survivor During the Holocaust] (Jerusalem, 1984). On this topic, see the quote from R. Kotler in "*Halakhti MeAdam LeAdam*" [I Went From Person to Person], *Ha'aretz* (Oct 8, 1999), p. b6. Efraim Zuroff's work on Va'ad Hatzalah, *The Response of Orthodox Jewry in the United States to the Holocaust* (New York, 2000) appeared after completion of this essay, and includes references to a number of letters to and from R. Kotler.

Shmuel Mirsky, *Mosedot Torah BeEropah BeVinyanam UveHurbanam* [European Torah Institutions: Their Building and Destruction] (New York, 1956) contains short articles about numerous European yeshivas, including Hillel Ziedmans article on the yeshivas in Slutzk and Kletzk, pp. 229-242. Information about the yeshiva, as well as personal memoirs and photographs, appear in the memorial volumes for the communities of Slutzk and Kletzk: *Pinqas Slutzk UVenotehah*, edited by N. Chinutz (Tel Aviv, 1962), and *Pinqas Kletzk*, edited by A. S. Stein (Tel Aviv, 1959). Akiva Egozi, "*Beit Midrash Gavoha Be-Lakewood*," *Shevilei Hinnukh*, Vol. 22 (Fall, 1962), pp. 120-124 contains information about the yeshiva in Lakewood around the time of R. Kotler's death. The Lakewood yeshiva published a fiftieth anniversary volume, which includes some of the above articles, as well as other useful material, *Beth Medrash Govoha: The Birth of a New Torah World*, edited by Menachem Lubinsky (Lakewood, 1992). William Helmreich's sociological study of the American yeshiva discusses R. Kotler, the yeshiva in Lakewood, and American yeshivas in general. See *The World of the Yeshiva* (New York, 1982). Shaul Stampfer describes the social history of Lithuanian yeshivas in the nineteenth century in his *HaYeshivah HaLita'it BeHithavutah* [The Development of the Lithuanian Yeshiva] (Jerusalem, 1995).

I was able to interview a number of students from Kletzk and Lakewood, as well as a few of R. Kotler's personal acquaintances: R. Avigdor Affen, who studied with Kotler in Vilna and outlying cities during World War II, in Jerusalem on July 22, 1999; R. Dr. Moshe Chigier, who studied in Slutzk and Kletzk, in Jerusalem on July 25, 1999; R. Asher Katz, one of the first students in Lakewood, by telephone to Brooklyn, New York, on July 26, 1999; R. Nachum Zeides, a student in Kletzk, Vilna, and Lakewood, by telephone to Lakewood on July 29, 1999; R. Dr. Yoel Ungar, a former student in Lakewood, by telephone to Denver, Colorado, on September 8, 1999; R. Joseph Maza, a student in Lakewood during the 1940s, by telephone to South River, New Jersey, on September 21, 1999; R. Akiva Egozi, a student in Kletzk, Vilna, and Lakewood, by telephone to Miami, Florida, on October 4, 1999; and Mrs. Shirley Lerner, a Lakewood resident at the time when the yeshiva was founded, in Beit Shemesh, Israel, on July 7, 2001. Chigier published his memoirs in both English and Hebrew: *Sam Hayyim* [The Spice of Life] (Jerusalem, n.d.) and *Slutzk, Johannesburg, Jerusalem* (Pittsburgh, 1992). (I would like to thank David Eisen for introducing me to this fascinating man.)

Three volumes of R. Kotler's public lectures were published by students under the title, *Mishnat Rabbi Aharon* [The Thought of Rabbi Aharon] (Lakewood, N.J.). I refer to the 1996 edition, which differs from other editions only slightly in pagination and content. These volumes contain virtually no bibliographical information. When were the lectures given? Before which audience? Are they transcripts or student notes? How were they edited and prepared for publication? Which lectures were chosen for publication, and based on what criteria? What else is available? The fact that the essay, "Preparation for Torah Study," was expurgated from later versions—perhaps because it admits some measure of historical change in the method of traditional Talmud study—points to a measure of self-censorship on the part of the editors. Selections from R. Kotler's open letters urging people to vote for the Agudat Yisrael party in Israeli elections appear in *Quntres Milhamtah Shel Torah* [A Pamphlet on the War of Torah] (Benei Berak, 1977). A few other essays and open letters appear in an undated *Quntres Keter Torah* [Pamphlet on the Crown of Torah] (n.p., n.d.). Some of these essays are reprinted in *Mishnat Rabbi Aharon*. *Sefer HaKenesiyah HaGedolah* [The Book of the Great Assembly], edited by Moshe Akiva Druck (Jerusalem, 1980) contains short excerpts from a few of his addresses to Agudat Yisrael conventions. Quite a few volumes of halakhic responsa and Talmudic novelae were published in a number of editions, also under the title *Mishnat Rabbi Aharon* (Lakewood). I intend to discuss the ideological content of R. Kotler's thought in my forthcoming doctoral dissertation at The Hebrew

University of Jerusalem, which will address the relationship between private religion and secular public culture in American Jewish thought.

There may be other relevant information scattered in the European Yiddish press, in the archives of Vaad HaYeshivot, Agudat Yisrael, Beth Medrash Govoha, as well as in R. Kotler's files in the Lakewood archives. (Bunim refers to these private archives, but I was unable to gain access to them.) According to Marvin Schick, a student of R. Kotler, many of the pre-war records and correspondence were destroyed in Vilna. He suggests fuller examination of the material available in the YIVO archives (Schick, "*Rav Aharon Lo Meit,*" p. 83).

4. Shaul Stampfer and Emmanuel Etkes dispute whether there was or was not any crisis at the time Volozhin was founded. See Stampfer, *HaYeshiva*, 35ff, and Emmanuel Etkes, "*Shitato UFo'alo Shel R. Hayyim Volozhin KeTeguvat HaHevrah HaMitnagdit LeHasidut*" [The Theory and Actions of R. Hayyim Volozhin as a Response of the Mitnagdic Society to Hasidism], *Proceedings of the American Academy of Jewish Research*, Vol. 38–39 (1972), pp. 1–45.

5. On R. Meltzer, see Aaron Rothkoff, "Rav Isser Zalman Meltzer," *Jewish Life*, Vol. 38, No. 4 (1971), pp. 50–57.

6. R. Kotler discusses this period in his eulogy for R. Meltzer, *Mishnat Rabbi Aharon*, Vol. 3, pp. 204–210.

7. I suspect that it is not accidental that R. Meltzer wrote a letter in support of the memorial volume for the town of Kletzk (*Pinqas Kletzk*, p. 15), even though he spent very little time there, while no such letter from R. Kotler appears. R. Meltzer was considerably closer to the simple, common Jew than R. Kotler was.

8. Chinutz, *Pinqas Slutzk*, p. 110.

9. Chigier, *Slutzk, Johannesburg, Jerusalem*, pp. 41–42.

10. On the Va'ad Hatzalah, see Zuroff, *The Response of Orthodox Jewry*.

11. Charles Liebman, "Orthodoxy in American Jewish Life," *American Jewish Year Book*, Vol. 66 (1965), pp. 93–97, and *Birth of a New Torah World* (unpaginated), last page.

12. Zeidman in Mirsky, *Mosedot Torah BeEropah*, p. 235 indicates that in 1939 the yeshiva numbered 260 students between ages 17 and 28 or older. Simha Gordon (in *Pinqas Kletzk*, p. 40), apparently based on the same source as Zeidman, if not on Zeidman himself, probably means "55 students above age 25" instead of the "55 students age 25." *Pinqas Kletzk*, p. ב, includes a group photograph of the Yeshiva students and administration.

13. On life in the town of Kletzk, see "Kletzk," *Encyclopedia Judaica*, (Jerusalem, 1972), Vol. 10, col. 1106–1107; "Kletzk," from the Beit HaTefutzot Community Database; *Pinqas Kletzk*, passim. Interviews with former residents supported the information available from these sources.

14. Stein, *Pinqas Kletzk*, p. 41. Chigier, *Slutzk, Johannesburg, Jerusalem*, pp. 17–21. Interviews with Chigier, Zeides, and Egozi. Zeidman indicates that the students organized a committee to standardize and lower housing prices, similar to the committee in Telz (Zeidman in Mirsky, *Mosedot Torah BeEropah*, p. 238. Cf. Stampfer, *HaYeshiva*, pp. 265–266). On the role of the dormitory in creating closed yeshivas, see below and Shaul Stampfer, "*HaPenimiyah VehaYeshivah BeMizrah Eropah*" [The Dormitory and the Yeshiva in Eastern Europe], in *HaHinnukh HaPenimiyati HaMamlakhti-Dati BeYisrael* [Dormitories in Reli-

gious Public Schools in Israel], edited by Matityahu Dagan (Jerusalem, 1997), pp. 20-31.

15. Stein, *Pinqas Kletzk*, p. 41.

16. As might be expected, there was some tension between R. Kotler and the local community rabbi, although the rabbi did not oppose construction of the yeshiva's new building. Cf. Stampfer, *HaYeshiva*, pp. 142-144. I did not find substantiation for the incident of *malshinut* which Galerentler reports (*Maran HaGaon Rabbi Aharon Kotler Zt"l*, p. 11).

17. On the kehillah in Poland at the time, see Gershon C. Bacon, *The Politics of Tradition: Agudat Yisrael in Poland, 1916-1939* (Jerusalem, 1996), pp. 178-224. Robert Moses Shapiro, "The Polish Kehillah Elections of 1936: A Revolution Re-examined," *Polin*, Vol. 8 (1994), pp. 206-226. Idem, "Jewish Communal Politics in Transition: The Vilna Kehile, 1919-1920," *YIVO Annual*, Vol. 20 (1991), pp. 61-91. Samuel D. Kassow, "Community and Identity in the Interwar Shtetl," in *The Jews of Poland Between the Two World Wars*, edited by Yisrael Gutman *et al.* (Hanover, London, 1989), pp. 198-220.

18. Sorsky, *Marbitzei Torah UMusar*, p. 270.

19. On R. Kotler's fundraising trip to the U. S. see Galerentler, *Maran HaGaon Rabbi Aharon Kotler Zt"l*, p. 6 and Pekier, *Reb Aharon*, pp. 72-74.

20. Although, as Stampfer notes, we require further research on how the presence of a yeshiva might influence a small town financially, socially, and intellectually ("*HaPenimiyah VehaYeshivah*," n. 23).

21. Stein, *Pinqas Kletzk*, p. 41.

22. Stein, *Pinqas Kletzk*, p. א shows a photograph of the town's kehillah with R. Kotler in the center. Pekier, *Reb Aharon*, p. 64, explains that in Europe he "allowed himself to be photographed in the company of the secularists to show 'that we are a force to be reckoned with. We will not be pushed aside or ignored! We must be represented in the kehillah so that we may be able to refute the false claims of the secular and show them the error of their ways.'" Pekier does not indicate a source for this quote. In general, R. Kotler thoroughly opposed non-Orthodox Jews in positions of leadership. See the excerpts from his speech at the Agudat Yisrael convention in 1937, in *Sefer HaKenesiyah HaGedolah*, pp. 80-81.

23. Bacon, *Politics*, pp. 178-224, p. 182 in particular. On the same attitude in a slightly earlier period, see his "Prolonged Erosion, Organization and Reinforcement: Reflections on Orthodox Jewry in Congress Poland (up to 1914)," in *Major Changes Within the Jewish People in the Wake of the Holocaust*, edited by Yisrael Gutman (Jerusalem, 1996), pp. 71-91, pp. 81ff in particular.

24. Interviews with Chigier, Zeides, and Egozi. Also see Kassow, *The Jews of Poland*, p. 211.

25. Interviews with Chigier and Egozi.

26. "נייר אשר יצר", from "*Halakhti MeAdam LeAdam*."

27. Interviews with Katz, Zeides, Egozi, and Lerner. Maza indicated that his involvement with local Jewish concerns, attempting to found a Jewish day school, was the rare exception among Lakewood students. He did so only because he had young children who required education.

28. R. Kotler, *Mishnat Rabbi Aharon*, Vol. 1, p. 35; Vol. 3, pp. 152-156, 187, 195, 216.

29. On Interwar Orthodoxy, see Jenna Weissman Joselit, *New York's Jewish Jews: The Orthodox Community in the Interwar Years* (Bloomington, 1990). The quote is from, p. xiii. Also see Jeffery Gurock's, *American Jewish Orthodoxy in Historical Perspective* (Hoboken NJ, 1996).

30. These quotes come from R. Kotler, *Mishnat Rabbi Aharon*, Vol. 3, pp. 154-155, 189, and 216-217. Helmreich reports that R. Kotler refused invitations to speak at Yeshiva University, *The World of the Yeshiva*, p. 41 n. 56.

31. R. Kotler considered gentiles spiritually irrelevant. See *Mishnat Rabbi Aharon*, Vol. 3, p. 92.

32. See above, n. 27.

33. Erving Goffman, *Asylums: Essays on the Social Situation of Mental Patients and Other Inmates* (Garden City, 1961), p. xiii. Much of Goffman's analysis depends on conflict and tension between inmates and staff. Yeshivas certainly suffer considerably less from this problem than psychiatric asylums, prisons, boot camps, and concentration camps.

34. R. Kotler, *Mishnat Rabbi Aharon*, Vol. 1, pp. 146-149, 197-198, 217 indicate that students should never leave yeshiva. Vol. 1, p. 220 accepts that some students should leave eventually, and R. Kotler had urged some of the students with whom I spoke to become communal rabbis and teachers.

35. Interviews with Katz, Zeides, and Maza.

36. Helmreich, *The World of the Yeshiva*, p. 43; Pekier, *Reb Aharon*, pp. 143-145; Sorsky, *Marbitzei Torah Umusar*, pp. 263-4; Lubinsky, *Birth of a New Torah World*, Tribute to Charles Gamal, [unpaginated]; Bunim, *A Fire in His Soul*, pp. 201, 215.

37. Helmreich, *The World of the Yeshiva*, p. 40.

38. See above, n. 36, and Bunim, *A Fire in His Soul*, pp. 213-216. Space considerations prevent a fuller discussion of the subtle messages in his fund-raising speeches, which appear in R. Kotler, *Mishnat Rabbi Aharon*, Vol. 3, pp. 20-22, 185-198.

39. See Solomon Poll, *The Hasidic Community of Williamsburg: A Study in the Sociology of Religion* (New York, 1962).

40. This changed to a great degree as the yeshiva grew, and its married students brought their families to Lakewood. Today, Lakewood maintains a thriving Haredi communal and economic life, which would make a fascinating sociological study.

41. I deal with this issue further in my forthcoming doctoral dissertation.

42. On Haskalah and Zionism in the Lithuanian yeshiva in general, see Stampfer, *HaYeshiva*, pp. 158ff, 170ff, 284ff, and Jacob J. Schachter, "Haskalah, Secular Studies, and the Close of the Yeshiva in Volozhin in 1892," *The Torah U-Madda Journal*, Vol. 2 (1990), pp. 76-132.

43. Chinutz, *Pinqas Slutzk*, pp. XXI-XXII.

44. Chigier, *Slutzk, Johannesburg, Jerusalem*, pp. 6, 74.

45. Rosenblum, *Reb Yaakov*, pp. 40-42; Pekier, *Reb Aharon*, pp. 26-27; Sorsky, *Marbitzei Torah Umusar*, Vol. 2, p. 219. Warhaftig, *Palit VeSarid BiYmei HaShoah*, p. 223, heard rumors that R. Kotler had actually dabbled in Haskalah for a short time, which only made him more wary of its dangers.

46. Stein, *Pinqas Kletzk*, pp. 132-137

47. Warhaftig, *Palit VeSarid BiYmei HaShoah*, p. 223.

48. Chigier reports that some students were active in Agudah, while other students indicated that there was virtually no student involvement in local political concerns. In R. Kotler's letter to Zerah Warhaftig, responding to the claim that Zionist students were being mistreated (Warhaftig, *Palit VeSarid BiYmei HaShoah*, p. 223), he stated that the yeshiva discourages student involvement in any organization, whether Agudat Yisrael or Mizrahi.

49. On college attendance, see Helmreich, *The World of the Yeshiva*, p. 220.

50. This came up in virtually all of my discussions with former Lakewood students.

51. On the ways in which American yeshivas had Americanized, see William Helmreich, *The World of the Yeshiva*, and Jeffery S. Gurock, *The Men and Women of Yeshiva: Higher Education, Orthodoxy, and American Judaism* (New York, 1988), Chapter 2 in particular.

52. Gurock, *American Orthodoxy*, pp. 299–312.

53. Liebman, "Orthodoxy," pp. 34–36.

Henry Wassermann

THE *WISSENSCHAFT DES JUDENTUMS* AND PROTESTANT THEOLOGY: A REVIEW ESSAY*

This highly interesting and original book is both sequel and supplement to *Christians and Jews in Germany–Religion, Politics and Ideology in the Second Reich, 1870–1914* (New York, 1971) by the late Professor Uriel Tal, one of the classics of modern Israeli historiography. At the same time, it is also an attempt to reply to the thesis formulated by Gerhard G. Scholem in his poignant 1962 article, *"Wider den Mythos vom deutsch-jüdischen Gespräch"* (Against the Myth of a German-Jewish Dialogue). The appended subtitle of Wiese's work, *Ein Schrei ins Leere?* (A cry into the void?), illustrates that no real dialogue or symbiosis has ever occurred between Germans and Jews and their cry for recognition has remained unanswered. Even though a large portion of the extensive historiography written about German-Jewish relations since the publication of that thesis seems overshadowed by its very impressive argumentation, Wiese has formulated one of the most brilliant and thorough attempts to answer the question hurled into the world by Scholem. Wiese has also managed to supply his answer with a surprising degree of self-assurance, thanks largely to the thematic and chronological conciseness and the intellectual depth of his analyses. This is indeed a thorough examination of the manner in which two communities of scholars—Jewish and Protestant theologians—who were members of the academic intelligentsia of pre-World War I Germany, both of which were relatively uniform—academically speaking—and characterized by both religious and national partisanship, reacted to each other. We are also offered a rare opportunity to get a close look at the intellectual entrails of our spiritual and professional forefathers, members of the second and third generations of *Wissenschaft des Judentums* in Germany, the *Urvater* of all contemporary academic Jewish Studies programs—some of whom were the mentors of our own learned teachers.

Wiese's leading question is: Did a dialogue take place between *Wissenschaft des Judentums* and Protestant theological research in a spirit of equality, respect, and mutual recognition, or was it merely a modern

---

*Christian Wiese, *Wissenschaft des Judentums und protestantische Theologie im wilhelminischen Deutschland–Ein Schrei ins Leere?* (Tübingen: Mohr Siebeck, 1999), xxvi + 507 pages.

version of the traditional literature of Jewish-Christian dispute and controversy? This main question leads to a multitude of intriguing secondary ones, also answered poignantly. Here are some of these questions, in his own phrasing: "How did the emancipation of Jews in Germany—which materialized gradually, but not without obstacles and manifestations of unwillingness to accept it—affect the controversy between the faiths and the cultural encounter between their adherents?"; "What is the significance of the *Wahrnehmung* (German for "acceptance," "perception," and mainly "appreciation")—in this case relating to the attitude of Protestant theology towards Judaism and Jews—in a situation where this theology, enjoying a dominant position under governmental patronage, insisted on its own religious supremacy and stressed its uniqueness as distinct from both historical and contemporary Judaism?"; "Did Jewish apologetics, which accompanied the demand for the acceptance of the findings of *Wissenschaft des Judentums* scholarship, arouse any reaction or did they remain unanswered?"; "How did Protestant theology, as the dominant discipline, react to the attempts of the Jewish community—which, while undergoing a process of self emancipation, argued that it could provide scientifically sound findings to justify its claims—to take part in describing and evaluating its own history?"

The first chapter, "The Political and Social Situation of the Jewish Community in Wilhelmine Germany from 1890 to 1914," presents the *dramatis personae* of the pending drama: the disintegration of the ideological affinity and bond between Jews and political Liberalism during the *Kulturkampf* (the struggle between Imperial Germany and the Catholic Church) initiated by Bismarck, and the spread of modern anti-Semitism; the process of accepting the fact that despite the Jews' legislative and constitutional emancipation, some barriers and hurdles remained insurmountable; the fact that simultaneously with the "assimilation crisis," various trends for reevaluatingng Judaism also appeared, manifested in the formulation of a "German-Jewish subculture," a new willingness for organized defensive actions against anti-Semitism involving a range of manifestations from *Trotzjudentum* (Judaism of remaining Jewish out of spite) to what is sometimes termed "a Jewish Renaissance" (usually referring to prolific journalistic activities, which—in our opinion—were generally bereft of content from a religious point of view); and finally, the growing influence of the new Zionist movement with its superficial neo-Romantic ideas—a typical example of that era's national movements—with few supporters, but it was vociferous and certain that it had the key to the succour of the Jewish People.

> The description so far has shown that the period between 1890 and 1914, from the point of view of the Jewish community, and based on the described political and social factors, was marked in particular by a Jewish identity crisis

and by the attempt (of this community) to define its place in German society. Attempts to answer the major questions—regarding the "religious" (*Konfessionellen*) or the "national" nature of Judaism, the legitimacy and significance of a "distinct Jewish consciousness" (*Sonderbewußtsein*), the possibility of coping with anti-Semitism by means of a convincing description of the value of Jewish faith and culture—all these attempts make it possible to identify a characteristic trend: A clearly and constantly expanding Jewish consciousness, combined with a growing demand—despite all efforts to increase integration [into the German environment]—that the contribution of Judaism to "Germanness" (*Deutschtum*) must be heard and combined with the attainment of political, legislative, social and institutional equality for the Jewish community (p. 57-58).

The second chapter, "Self-understanding and the Research Conditions of *Wissenschaft des Judentums*," provides a thorough and comprehensive presentation of the institutional history of *Wissenschaft des Judentums* in Germany and a description of the three rabbinical seminaries, at which *Wissenschaft des Judentums* was established, developed, and consolidated in accordance with the three dominant confessional movements of German Jewry (Reform and Othodoxy in Berlin and Conservative—for lack of another term—in Breslau). The core of the chapter describes the conditions under which the encounter between *Wissenschaft des Judentums* and Protestant theology took place—both in terms of the tension between institutional discrimination dictated by the state and the demand of the same institutions for acknowledging the contribution of *Wissenschaft des Judentums*, and in terms of the role of *Wissenschaft des Judentums* in the struggle against anti-Semitism.

A precise and interesting manifestation of the attitudes prevailing within the new Jewish academic-Rabbinical intelligentsia may be found in Rabbi Dr. Joseph Ecshelbacher's "Statement about a Proposal [formulated by Rabbi Dr. Ismar Elbogen c. 1908], for establishing a Supervisory Committee for New Publications which concern Jews and Judaism in any way":

> It is an act necessitated by our self-respect as well as part and parcel of the struggle for truth, that steps be taken against these attitudes of disrespect and simple disregard. We do not wish to force an opinion upon anyone, but we do want to be heard and respected. All we want is to offer the world the raw materials necessary for a careful and comprehensive examination to make a fair judgment possible. We want to make sure that the works of talented, knowledgeable and inspired Jewish writers cease gathering dust, totally ignored, in book shops, but rather that they receive the reading and appreciation they deserve by Jews and by serious and truth-loving non-Jews alike (p. 84).

The third chapter, "*Wissenschaft des Judentums*s and the Protestant 'Mission to the Jews' from 1880 to 1914," analyzes the personal encounters—usually tense and loaded with contradiction—between leaders of *Wissenschaft des Judentums* and heads of the Protestant Mission to the Jews movement, who, in the 1880s, 1890s and the early years of the twentieth century raised a brave voice against anti-Semitic agitation. This encounter is associated with the names of three Protestant scholars and theologians who were among the first to show appreciation for Rabbinical and Talmudic sources: Gustav Dalman (1855–1941), Franz Delitzsch (1811–1890), and Hermann L. Strack (1848–1922). Both Delitzsch and Strack established an *Institutum Judaicum*, in Leipzig and Berlin, primarily for improving the training of missionaries to the Jews by acquainting them with Jewish sources, mainly from the times of the Mishna and Talmud—but also for spreading a true picture of Judaism as part of the struggle against anti-Semitism.

As might have been expected, the relations were inevitably tense. Leaders of the Jewish community were forced to exercise considerable restraint toward the well-wishing newcomers, as may be construed from the title of an article written in 1883, dealing with Delitzsch's rather ambivalent attitude towards the Talmud: "We must not hurt the hand benevolently stretched out toward us."

> On the other hand, he [Delitzsch] in particular understood the task of the study of Judaism by Christianity first and foremost in the sense of "an apologetic of Christianity directed towards Jews" and as a "a Christian criticism of Judaism based upon scholarly-scientific findings." The aim was to act in a mission-oriented manner against the role of *Wissenschaft des Judentums* in unifying and strengthening Jewish identity. In the name of a dominant religion and science, a theologian like Delitzsch spoke with Jewish researchers who—as Jews—insisted upon their [religious] truth regarding the history of Salvation only in the very ancient [Biblical] past or in the very distant [eschatological] future. From these viewpoints their present Jewish identity seemed [to Deltizsch] to be a self-delusion. The Jewish scholars, on their part, had to acknowledge the fact that, at least initially, they were taken seriously as scholars and researchers. But as Jews they were degraded to the level of objects whose religious loyalty was an impediment which must be overcome. Recognizing them as equals, as *Jewish* scholars and as representatives of a legitimate Jewish community, was beyond the intentions of the Protestant "Missionaries to the Jews": Their "Love of Israel" was primarily directed toward Jews as potential Christians (p. 130).

The fourth chapter, "The Controversy about the Description of Pharisee-Rabbinical Judaism in New Testament Historiography between 1900 and 1914," opens with a presentation of the series of influential lectures given by the important theologian Adolph von Harnack (1851–1930) on *Wesen des Christentums (Essence of Christianity)* at Berlin University during winter semester 1899–1900. In these lectures Harnack claimed *inter alia* that Jesus had summed up everything of value in the Jewish faith in his teachings, whereas Judaism had continued stagnating under the influence of the Rabbis, Priests, and Pharisees. This picture was no more and no less than a "scientific" confirmation of the traditional "truth" of Christian theology about the transference of the Election from Judaism to the "New Israel," Christianity. This position, which prevented any possible dialogue with Judaism, was perceived as a grave insult by about a dozen Rabbis of the time, who took the trouble to respond immediately and in great detail. The most prominent among them were: Leo Baeck (1873-1956), Ismar Elbogen (1874-1943), Moritz Güdemann (1835-1918), Joseph Eschelbacher (1848-1916), and Felix Perles (1874-1933), Rabbi of Königsberg, who also taught at the local university (and eventually received an honorary professorship in 1924).

The major part of the chapter discusses Felix Perles' incisive criticism of Wilhelm Bousset (1865-1920), the principal representative of the group of influential scholars who were pioneering the study of religions by means of the historical method. In his monumental study of 1903, *Religion des Judentums im neutestamentlichen Zeitalter (The Jewish Religion in the New Testament Period)*, Bousset had presented the emergence of Christianity according to the historical method of source criticism, and had announced "the absolute supremacy of the Christian religion over all other religions." He repeated this principle several times, finally giving it a Hegelian phrasing, stating that Christianity is "the clearest expression of everything that has struggled to take shape in the long history of religion" (p. 145).

According to Bousset, Judaism had been a national-particularistic ritualistic religion, which thanks to Babylonian and Persian influences, had developed universal tendencies, but had stopped halfway. A new development had therefore become necessary, and had been manifested in the figure of Christ, who was much greater than both the Jewish visionaries predicting Judgment Day and the figures who had formulated Rabbinical-Pharisee theology. Jesus had saved some dormant embers from the rich but decomposing "Late Judaism" (*Spätjudentum*) of the Second Temple period, and had transformed them into a vibrant religious movement. He had been both a teacher and a prophet, who, with his personal power alone, had created a new religion and put an end to the old one. The use of the expression "Late Judaism," fraught as it was with multiple meanings, indicated that Bousset had admitted that some homage should be paid to Judaism as the incubator of Christianity; this homage, however, was based upon the belief that the Prophets had been the highest and ultimate achievement of Judaism, and that what had followed was an unstoppable process of stagnation and decline.

Perles criticized the array of sweeping generalizations and characterizations employed by Bousset to demean "Late Judaism"—which were based upon his alleged proficiency in rabbinical sources—with one of the most effective of an academic's weapons, sheer sarcasm:

> What would we have said if a German professor at an institution of higher education, who could not read even one page of the [ancient Greek] sources, had dared to write a description of [Greek] philosophy which claimed to be a work of scholarship, but was based solely upon translations of works [of the ancient Greek philosophers], such as *apopthegms* [in Greek letters, i. e. anthologies of summaries] of the sayings of the most important philosophers, while blindly relying upon *Die Philosophie der Griechen* (*The Philosophy of the Greeks* [a work of historical synthesis]) by [Eduard] Zeller? *(Bousset's Religion des Judentums: im neutestamentlichen Zeitalter kritisch untersucht* [Berlin, 1903]).

Bousset responded bluntly:

> If he insists on hearing it: I cannot view the continued existence of Judaism in its Talmudic form as having any value or purpose in its own right, in the higher sense of the word. And I cannot count the Mishna and Gemara among the treasures of human spiritual life, which would be irreplaceable if lost (p. 154).

Most of Bousset's colleagues among the Protestant theologians of the time found that Perles' essay was saturated with hatred, nationalistic bigotry, and insolence. His friend and pupil, Professor Hugo Gressmann congratulated him with, "I am glad you hit that Jew smack in the face *(Schnauze)* as he had it coming." But Bousset himself did something very rare in academic circles in general, and among German Protestant theologians in particular: he subjected himself to a process of self-criticism and learning. In the second edition of his book he softened his negative criticism and praised hidden aspects of the faith of Israel, particularly those found in Hebrew prayers (but without mentioning Perles' name even once!).

Moreover, in 1915, in the midst of World War I—which at its start brought patriotic German and Jewish hearts closer together again— Bousset wrote an enthusiastic review of Ismar Elbogen's very important 1913 study, *Der jüdische Gottesdienst in seiner geschichtlichen Entwicklung (Jewish Services in their Historical Development)*. He praised the book emphatically and used it as a basis for criticizing studies by his colleagues as well as by himself with regard to the importance of the influence of Jewish prayer on the formation of Christianity. He even admitted that the central Christian prayer, "Our Father," had emerged from the language of the Pharisees, and added: "In this respect . . . I see myself, in addition, as guilty, and apply this criticism to my own work, *The Jewish Religion*."

The fifth chapter, "The Jewish *Wahrnehmung* of Protestant Old Testament Research and of its Evaluation of the Hebrew Bible between 1900 and 1914," examines five responses of Jewish academic scholars to the challenge of the new method of studying the Hebrew Bible known as Higher Source Criticism and introduced by Julius Wellhausen (1844–1918). This method captured German academia by storm and could not be ignored by the many rabbis who were writing dissertations at German universities in order to obtain the required double titles of *Herr Dr. Rabbiner*. One interesting reaction was provided by Benno Jacob (1862–1945), Rabbi of Dortmund, who had devoted decades to monumental commentaries on the books of Genesis and Exodus (translated into English in 1974 and 1992 but not yet into Hebrew), in an effort to develop a "Jewish" Hebrew Bible research that would counterbalance destructive Higher Source Criticism. As early as 1898 he wrote:

> The only thing created by the Jewish nation, which is one of the immortal assets that bring happiness to the world, the basis for its spiritual life which has existed for three thousand years, its superior good, the thing that is most sacred to it—this has been taken away from it by force. Our Bible is no longer our Bible [...]. We need a Science of the Bible (*Bibelwissenschaft*), that will not only determine what is right, but will also "refresh the soul," will not only be truthful, but will "make the ignorant wise," will not only be accurate but "will make hearts rejoice," will not only be free of error, but will also "open the eyes of the blind." Only such research is appropriate for the real essence of the Bible, and hence—it must be admitted that understanding the Bible is something which can be accomplished ... only by a Jew (pp. 184; 185).

Was this passage written a hundred years ago or yesterday?

Another challenge from this direction arose during the course of a lawsuit filed by the *Central-Verein*, the large Jewish defense organization fighting against anti-Semitism. The suit was filed against the anti-Semitic agitator T. Fritzsch (1852–1933) who had been prosecuted several times and usually lost in court. In 1911 he was sued for publishing a venomous booklet called *Beweis-Material gegen Jahwe (Evidence-Material against Jehova)*, in which he tried to prove that the Jewish religion had become "the curse of contemporary culture because of its malicious and humanity-hating spirit." The German Supreme Court in Leipzig granted Fritzsch's attorneys' request that professional opinions be submitted before considering the complaint. Both sides recruited a number of learned professors, and therefore the court asked the renowned authority in Old Testament studies, Professor Dr. Rudolf Kittel (1853–1929) of the University of Leipzig, to present a decisive, final opinion. Kittel's report, after considerable hesitation, vacillation, and declarations of repugnance towards Fritsch, aborted the complaint against him by confirming that the idea of the inferiority of Old Testament Jewish morality had been accepted by contemporary Old Testament scholars. Fritzsch used Kittel's verdict exhaustively in his propaganda.

The sixth chapter, "The Legitimacy of Judaism's Continued Existence—the Political Dimension of the Controversy between Liberal Judaism and Liberal Protestantism in the Context of the Internal Jewish Identity Disputes, 1900–1914," is, to my mind, the pinnacle of the entire work. The chapter presents the dilemma of the German Jewish Liberal *Bildungsbürgertum* (the bourgeoisie based upon educational and cultural values best exemplified by the German concepts of *Kultur* and *Bildung*) which, at the height of its assimilation process—aiming from the outset to resemble the Protestant academic *Bildungsbürgertum* (also known as *Kulturprotestantismus*)—tried to answer the essential question: in which ways were highly-assimilated German Jews still Jews? *Wissenschaft des Judentums*s was charged with finding as answer to a challenge, aptly formulated by the eminent scholar of the history of Jewish philosophy, J. Guttman, in 1910:

> A certain trend in modern theology deprives Judaism—in the name of science—of its right to exist. Its purpose is to obscure the contents of Judaism, and after doing so it attributes all achievements in the cultural life of humanity to Christianity alone, obliterating the contribution of Judaism (p. 240).

Here controversy was especially bitter—as Uriel Tal had already observed—because of the deep resemblance between the theologies of Liberal Judaism and of Liberal Protestantism. We cannot here present in detail all the disputes, described by Wiese with considerable talent, apart from the one that was perhaps the most bitter of all: the debate between Reform Judaism and Orthodox Judaism as exemplified by its sharp-tongued representative, Rabbi Prof. Dr. Joseph Wohlgemuth (1867–1942), head of the Orthodox Rabbinical Seminary in Berlin. Wohlgemuth had already noticed the signs of growing a resemblance between Liberal Judaism and Liberal Protestantism, and he used the self-identifying definitions of Liberal Judaism to expel it from the ranks of Judaism altogether: Liberal Judaism had adopted the distinction between a universal prophetic religion and a religion based on operative commandments (*Mitzvot*) from Protestant theology and had even consecrated the very same principles of faith, such as viewing the idea of monotheism and universal moral commands as the dominant aspect of religion. Wohlgemuth relentlessly exposed the fact that the attitude of Liberal Judaism to Jews who observed all the ritual commandments was basically parallel to the negative attitude of Liberal Protestantism to Judaism. The exposure of this truth only intensified the internal Jewish controversy.

Wiese's summation may be applied not only to the controversy between Liberal Protestant theology and Liberal Jewish theology, but also to other intellectual and academic disputes as well:

> The polemical debate about the spiritual similarity between the two Liberal movements was determined by complex apologetic interests. The two "conversing parties" did not truly confront each other but rather reinforced their own identities by commenting upon and and interpreting that of their rival. Their similarity was such that it had to be perceived as a threat, and so much so, that they felt compelled to stress the differences between them with increasing clarity. States of theological uncertainty and indeterminancy within the ranks of each of both sides strengthened this tendency: Among the (Liberal)

Jewish scholars it was their ambivalent attitude towards the normative nature of Halacha and among the Protestant theologians it was the tension between loss of faith in the probability of Christological salvation dogma and in the uniqueness of Christ's teachings, which found their compensation in diminishing the importance of ancient Judaism by means of studying the history of the development of religions. The conflict intensified as a result of the criticism hurled at each side by conservative opposition from within: The Jewish-Orthodox critical attitude towards the "historization" of religious tradition caused by critical historical scholarship—which seemed to be aimed at shaking the traditional foundations of faith—reached its peak with the accusation that liberal Judaism was abandoning the true identity of the Jewish faith in the sense of a "Christianization" (*Christianisierung*) [of Judaism]. Whereas, on the other side, the excessive willingness of Liberal Protestant theology to pronounce all Jewish history after the Coming of Christ as totally *passé* and irrelevant, was further reinforced because their conservative opponents within the Church considered the minimalization of traditional Christology by the Liberal theologians as a sort of "Judaization" (*Judaisierung*) of Christianity. (p. 290f.)

In the seventh and final chapter, "The Acceptance of *Wissenschaft des Judentums*s by Academic Protestant Theology, 1900–1914," the frequency and force of reactions and counter-reactions between Rabbis representing *Wissenschaft des Judentums* and Protestant theologians and scholars—in both Jewish and German publications—reach such an intensity, that in our opinion they cannot be deprived of the title of constituting a "dialogue"—both German-Jewish and Jewish-Christian. Wiese, however, tries very hard to deny this. We chose to present here only a few of the cases attesting to the beginnings of a new willingness for a *Wahrnehmung* of *Wissenschaft des Judentums*.

In 1912, for example, the New Testament scholar Oscar Holtzman (1859–1932) of Giessen University, and the Old Testament scholar Georg Beer of Heidelberg initiated a very ambitious research project: publishing the whole of the Mishna in German translation, and accompanied by a scientific apparatus in the finest tradition of classical German philology. They started this project from a state of nearly total ignorance, blatantly ignoring—methodologically and conceptually—both the achievements of *Wissenschaft des Judentums* (Zacharias Frankel [1801–1875]!) as well as generations of traditional Jewish commentary on the Mishna. The initial achievements of the project—as expressed in the rapid publication of a large number of tractates—damaged its scientific reputation severely. In the view of its fiercest critic, Rabbi Professor Dr. Victor (Avigdor) Aptowitzer (1871–1932) of the Rabbinical Seminary in Vienna, Prof. Beer's attempt to prepare a critical-scientific edition of tractate *Pessachim* was no more and no less than "a document giving evidence of hatred and polemics against Judaism and the Jews, wrapped in cheap scientific silver wrapping paper, which gradually turns into a sanctimonious missionary sermon."

Further evidence for this willingness and openness can be found in the fact that on the eve of World War I several concrete proposals were presented for employing Yeshiva-trained scholars in academic teaching positions. But only one of these proposals was actually put into effect, that of Prof. Rudolf Kittel, who in 1912 proposed appointing Israel Isser Kahan (1858-1924)—an observant Jew from Lithuania who had been one Delitzsch's assistants in the translation of the New Testament into Mishna-style Hebrew, an experienced teacher at the *Institutum Judaicum* for training missionaries, and Kittel's own close aide in the preparation of the early (and disappointing!) editions of the *Biblia Hebraica*—to the position of "lector," namely teaching assistant of "the Sciences of late Hebrew, Jewish-Aramaic and the Talmud" (*späthebräische, jüdisch-aramäische und talmudische Wissenschaft*). This was the first appointment of its kind in Germany, but it was somewhat spoiled by one of the arguments employed by Kittel:

> Here the serious danger arises, that where Christians may want to express their views on these issues, they will be forced to ask the advice of Jews. Furthermore, these fields of knowledge may gradually become a kind of **secret science** [emphasis in the original, H. W.]—an even more grievous threat, since lately a Jewish-apologetic trend, namely an aggressive anti-Christian trend, has been acquiring force within Judaism—much more so than in the past (p. 328).

We cannot describe in detail here the diminishing opposition to the establishment of faculties and professorial positions for *Wissenschaft des Judentums*s at German universities. We do, however, wish to point out that the proposal for establishing a Jewish-Theological faculty at the new university in Frankfurt am Main was not implemented, mostly, it seems, due to what Franz Rosenzweig described in a letter to Martin Buber in 1923: "(The reason, which the Christian initiators expected least of all, of course), was that the Jewish initiators and donors of the university thwarted the idea due to the familiar apprehension of 'don't be too Jewish (*nur nicht zu jüdisch*)'" (p. 345).

Another noteworthy initiative was that of Max Löhr (1864-1931), a professor of Old Testament studies at the University of Königsberg and a close friend of Rabbi Perles—and who regularly attended the local synagogue services. In the autumn of 1915, Löhr approached the famous Orientalist Theodor Nöldeke (1836-1930) to organize a memorandum for establishing a professorship in *Wissenschaft des Judentums* at a university in Prussia. He was able to obtain the signatures of twenty-seven professors—including Kittel and Wellhausen—on a memorandum which was presented in November 1915. The memorandum expressed desires identical with those formulated by Leopold Zunz (1794-1886) and Eduard Gans (1796-1839), the founders of the original "Association (*Verein*) for the Culture and *Wissenschaft des Judentums*" in Berlin almost 100 years earlier:

> The role of this professorial position will be studying the literature, history, theories and language of all post-Biblical Judaism, including that of the Middle Ages, according to the modern scientific method, while conducting fruitful mutual relations with the general world of knowledge *(universitas literarum)*, and also contributing to scientific activity which has regained official recognition, in order to spread in wide circles a more enlightened understanding of Judaism as an historically unique phenomenon (p. 350).

Unfortunately, the petitioners chose a bad time for presenting their proposal, and the memorandum wandered from one official to another for about ten years, until finally it disappeared altogether. The leaders of the *Wissenschaft des Judentums* found consolation in establishment an Academy for *Wissenschaft des Judentums* in 1919 in Berlin.

> The question about the encounter between Jewish research and Protestant theology, may be answered by trying to introduce real content into that "cry into an empty void"—in the words of the image used above. They [the Jewish scholars] presented to their Christian colleagues with their vision of a dialogue between Judaism and Christianity within German culture, which was perceived as pluralistic and in opposition to possessive claims, missionary intentions, and pretensions for exclusive ownership of the entire truth. They fought against the arrogance with which Protestant theologians silenced them, or ignored the fact that a living Judaism existed in their own time—demanding recognition of its own religious-cultural identity and its right to exist. They passionately disputed the hostile anti-Jewish tendencies of a theology, that seemed to endorse the distortion of Jewish tradition, and to characterize Judaism as an entity whose spirituality was totally contradictory to its own—in order to reinforce the claims of Christianity for total possession of the truth and the spirit of modernity. In order to cope with all this, the Jews tried to ask their Protestant colleagues to adopt a perspective of self-criticism and a scientific ethos. In terms of research, such an approach would depend on an unbiased acquaintance with Judaism, its sources, history and various forms of existence (through the ages)—and for this purpose, the Jews offered themselves as qualified partners in the proposed dialogue. They protested vehemently against theological discussions of Judaism—which either consciously aimed to create discrimination, or did not take into account their harmful effect in political contexts. They wished to form a solid front against anti-Semitism, which would be anchored in recognition of the common roots [of the two religions] and the threat posed to both by anti-Jewish animosity. Their underlying assumption was that each religion had the right to preserve its own identity, without disregarding the contrasts between them—all out of an open dialogue that would be more than a reflection of their respective political and social power. Finally, as they tried to understand Jesus and early Christianity in the context of the history of the Jewish faith, they created a **counter-history** [*Gegengeschichte*, highlighted in the original, H. W.], which totally contradicted the Christian interpretation of Christianity's beginnings, and was presented as a polemic challenge, and at the same time—a basis for dialogue (p. 363).

Strong words, which would certainly have made Scholem very happy. But in spite of my deep appreciation for the book—the result of extremely thorough research, evidenced by the bibliography of 1000 titles, well-organized indices and the biographical supplement (about a third of the book is composed of scholarly apparatus)—I am not certain that these are indeed the only possible conclusions to be drawn from Wiese's own findings. In fact, I doubt whether these conclusions should be assigned the high significance which he attributes to them.

With regard to these findings, it is difficult to understand why Bousset's learning process, the intriguing story of the Giessen Mishna project, the various initiatives for introducing the *Wissenschaft des Judentums* at German universities and other similar matters are not accepted by Wiese as evidence for the existence of any sort of dialogue. These findings were published simultaneously in Jewish, theological-Protestant and general scholarly periodicals, and formulated through mutual discussions within the Protestant and Jewish academic community. These communities read these periodicals with great interest. For example, the criticism of Aptowitzer (and other Jewish scholars) directed against the Giessen Mishna was examined, accepted, and as a result, competent Jewish scholars were recruited to join the project (which continues to this day!).

In addition, it is also difficult to understand how it could come about that, while Martin Buber (1978-1965) is mentioned six times, no mention is made of the fact that during the latter half of the period under review, Protestant theologians were becoming increasingly enamored of Buber's writings and, in particular, his writings on Hassidism (an affection which has faded, I believe, only amongst those with direct access to and acquaintance with Jewish sources). In later Wilhelmine Germany, Buber was, to a large degree, responsible for supplying Protestant theologians with a presentable and admirable picture of Judaism, one which many adopted willingly. Even if his writings cannot be defined as *Wissenschaft des Judentums* proper, ignoring his benign presence makes it much too easy for Wiese to advance his claims concerning the attitude of Protestant theology towards Judaism. The same holds true of the Nietzschean literary critic, author, and very fecund folklorist, M. J. Bin Gerion (Berdyczewski [1865-1921]), whose collections of Jewish legends, culled and adapted from all layers of rabbinical literature, were highly appreciated by Protestant scholars, as evinced in their admiring reviews of his collections (translated with great talent by his wife, Rahel), printed in good taste by a very popular publisher (*Insel*), and which are still available. Though some paragons of *Wissenschaft des Judentums* wrinkled their noses at his accomplishments, Bin Gerion definitely made an impact and made Jewish rabbinical literature accessible to Protestant scholars and theologians—the above-mentioned Hugo Gressmann was one of many who turned to him for advice—and his personal archive in Holon, Israel, contains scores of letters by leading Protestant scholars and theologians expressing their admiration. Bin Gerion is not mentioned at all, and neither are unique but interesting ventures such as the *Monumenta Talmudica* (Vienna and Leipzig, 1913).

Wiese points out, and rightly so, that the disputes between the representatives of the *Wissenschaft des Judentums*s and the representatives of Protestant theology were characterized by a lack of symmetry between a theology with an almost national status, under whose patronage great internationally acclaimed scientific achievements had been made, and the theology of a religion with no recognized status or prestige, whose followers numbered a mere 1.25 percent of the population. In this asymmetrical reality, Wiese does an extremely good job of exposing the disappointing intellectual and moral qualities of those he loves to hate—the liberal Protestant theologians, with their smooth, roundabout speech, who, while speaking ever so sweetly, aimed poisoned arrows at the Jews' most sensitive and vulnerable spots. But where did Wiese acquire the somewhat naive expectation that in intellectual-academic arguments, the wise and just—rather than the powerful—prevail? Had he given some consideration to the history and philosophy of science in general, and the structure of scientific-academic debates and disputes in particular, he would without doubt have lowered his intellectual-moral expectations. The world of learning, and particularly the world of academic learning, belongs to earth's imperfect reality.

Moreover, thanks to his evident and impressive analytic talents, Wiese has been able to unmask the intellectual and moral hypocrisy of the leading Protestant theologians in their attitude toward the *Wissenschaft des Judentums*s. This represented the spiritual leadership of German-speaking Jews in an era where they strove to become as Westernized and as Germanized as possible, and the prestige of science was at its peak, in a most fascinating manner. The book, however, also tries to buttress Scholem's most influential thesis. But even if we accept Wiese's conclusions about the lack of a German response to the Jews' cry into a void, that there was only a thunderous silence where German Jews had expected a willingness to conduct a dialogue, I doubt whether this silence can bear the burden of significance he assigns to it—as long as he ignores the fact that mutually attentive dialogues in situations of extremely asymmetrical social and political power, like in the case of Germans *vis-à-vis* German Jews—are extremely rare. Where was the Jews' cry for *Wahrnehmung* heard and replied to by Christians before they were murdered during World War II? In order to conduct any kind of Christian-Jewish dialogue, as it is sometimes conducted today, Christians—especially Protestants—had to lose some of their confidence in the absolute truth of their faith and their prospects of salvation, and this is something which occurred only a generation or two after the murder of the Jews of Europe by their German co-believers, namely, after the balance of faith, self-confidence, and power between the religions had shifted noticeably.

Wiese also believes that the fact that Protestant theology was not willing to respond to the cry of the *Wissenschaft des Judentums*s for recognition and equality in Wilhelmine Germany is significant with regard to the crimes committed by the Germans after the Nazis rose to power in 1933. As may be learned from the frequent use of the theologically-loaded word, *Shoah*—which is mentioned twelve times in the foreword, introduction, and epilogue—Wiese seems to believe that a burden of criminal responsibility should be borne by Wilhelmine academic Protestant theology for the murder of European Jewry committed a generation later because of its alleged silence, unresponsiveness, and unwillingness to hold a dialogue with *Wissenschaft des Judentums*. It is as though the genocide of the Jewish nation at a later date reflects guilt upon those Protestant theologians who had refused to conduct a fair dialogue a generation earlier. This fact reinforces, in his view, the significance of that empty void with which Protestant theology and scholarship allegedly presented towards the plaintive request of *Wissenschaft des Judentums* for dialogue and *Wahrnehmung*. I must express some skepticism here.

Wiese's accusations are much better grounded when he describes the assistance provided by Protestant theology, and especially scholars of the Old and New Testaments, all too frequently, to various manifestations of anti-Semitism. The son of Franz Delitzsch, Friedrich (1850–1922), a noted Assyrologist, for instance, became a professed anti-Semite and so did not a few of the first and second-generation students of the Protestant theologians discussed in the book; too many of them served Hitler willingly and enthusiastically. The most infamous, perhaps, was the son of Rudolf Kittel, Gerhard (1888–1948), a well-known scholar in his own right, and a pioneer in his positive appreciation of Rabbinical literature during the Weimar republic and who tried to establish a Nazified *Wissenschaft des Judentums* under the auspices of the Third Reich. But willingness to place intellectual resources at the service of national causes, as dark as they may be, and especially in wartime, has been a mark of the academic world since time immemorial, even in our own land—has it not? The problem lies not only in Wiese's attempt to lay blame and responsibility in a chronologically retrospective manner—fathers carry the blame for the deeds of the sons—but to lay extreme blame and culpability just for **silence** (and failure to respond to a cry for *Wahrnehmung*). But as is well known by every budding scholar—though rapidly forgotten in polemics and by ideologues—arguments *ex silentio* are often fraught with serious difficulties.

The empty void presented by the silence of powerful majorities in face of the outcry of powerless ethnic and religious minorities who long to be acknowledged as equals is as common today as it was in 1900—especially when those minorities have but little economic, political, or military power. There is certainly nothing unique about such a silence. The attribution of extreme guilt for murdering Jews when the issue is just silence and disregard is more than a bit problematic. When can one speak of a link of responsibility between the silence and disregard expressed by an academic intelligentsia, in command of an apparently scientific ideology as well as of claims fueled by deep religious and nationalistic beliefs, and the criminal actions (and inaction!) perpetrated by following generations? Always? One can only wish this was true, but I sincerely doubt it. What is the precise connection between the lack of *Wahrnehmung* demonstrated by the political theology of the early Central-European Zionist national movement before World War I toward the emerging "Arab question" in the Ottoman province of Palestine (if I remember correctly, the slogan rang, "A Land without People for a People without a Land") and the deportations (and even massacres) carried out in the midst of the bloody, fateful war of 1948? Do these later actions also stand in some causal relationship towards the initial silence?

I am not sure whether many readers will be willing to accept the ideas presented above. An approach close to that of Wiese, and which enhances the significance of human behavior patterns of non-Jews in general and of Germans in particular due to their connection or proximity with what is currently known as the Shoah, is most prevalent in our country. But I feel rather certain that most of us are aware that the outcry of a minority which is met with indifference, disregard, and silence of a majority is almost the way of the world since the days of Creation. I would prefer to refrain from enlarging upon culpability in such situations if only to avoid undue moralizing.

Moreover, do Wiese and Scholem, indeed, speak of anything that is more grievous than the silence of a powerful majority, complacent and revered, in the face of the cry of a small, venerating minority? And if one remembers the tenor of Scholem's very polemical article, this is the cry of a rejected lover, a lover who, hoping to win the heart of his beloved, has taken on that beloved's image and identity, and has lost himself completely in his new identity. This is the type of relationship which lies at the roots of Scholem's cry—the cry of that part of German Jewry which professed to reject its German cultural inheritance and rejoiced in adopting a new identity in Herzl's *Altneuland*—and which also gives a tragic dimension to the murder of German Jews by Germans, as noted by our teacher, the late Professor Jacob Katz: When the Germans murdered the Jews of Poland, Rumania, and the Ukraine, or the Jews of Thessaloniki and Lybia, they murdered victims who were distant and foreign to them. Thus, these terrible murders lack the real tragic dimension of the cases in which lives were taken by those whom the victims had striven to befriend and resemble.

The problem here is that reciprocal love is a relatively rare gift of grace. Perhaps, sometimes, it may be purchased at the price of self-effacement and coming to resemble the beloved—and there are many examples of this, on both the personal and public levels. But the rejection of love—especially love accompanied by self-effacement and the generation of an almost-identical resemblance—as painful as it is to the lover, does not necessarily taint the beloved with immoral qualities. The beloved's reaction may be interpreted, at the most, as obtuseness or insensitivity. Wiese's book contains evidence that various degrees of *Wahrnehmung* could be detected in the attitudes of Protestant theologians towards *Wissenschaft des Judentums*—even more so than it has become customary to admit today in the social history of relations between Germans and Jews. I believe that this fact adds a dimension of culpabilty and especially of tragedy to the murder of German Jews, and enhances the gravity of the crimes which were committed against them by those who had once been their fellow citizens, neighbors, colleagues and friends.

THE OPEN UNIVERSITY, ISRAEL

BOOKS RECEIVED*

Aaron, Rafi, *A Seed in the Pocket of Their Blood*. Syracuse University Press (Syracuse, 1997); 95 pp.
Auerbach, Jerold S., *Are We One? Jewish Identity in the United States and Israel*. Rutgers University Press (Piscataway, 2001); 248 pp.
Bauman, Zygmunt, *Modernity and the Holocaust*. Cornell University Press (Ithaca, 2000); 267 pp.
Bell, John, (ed.), *Puppets, Masks and Performing Objects*. New York University (New York, 2001); 197 pp.
Blumenthal, David R., *The Banality of Good and Evil: Moral Lessons from the Shoah and Jewish Tradition*. Georgetown University Press (Washington, 1999); 326 pp.
Burger, Naomi, and Alan L. Burger, (eds.), *Second Generation Voices: Reflections by Children of Holocaust Survivors and Perpetrators*. Syracuse University Press (Syracuse, 2001); 378 pp.
Chmiel, Mark, *Elie Wiesel and the Politics of Moral Leadership*. Temple University Press (Philadelphia, 2001); 225 pp.
Coogan, Michael D., (ed.), *The Oxford History of the Biblical World*. Oxford University Press (Oxford, 2001); 487 pp.
Diner, Hasia R., *Lower East Side Memories: A Jewish Place in America*. Princeton University Press (Princeton, 2001); 219 pp.
Dollinger, Marc, *Quest for Inclusion: Jews and Liberalism in Modern America*. Princeton University Press (Princeton, 2001); 296 pp.
Efron, John M., *Medicine and the German Jews: A History*. Vail-Ballou Press (Binghampton, 2001); 343 pp.
Finkelstein, Norman, *Not One of Them in Place: Modern Poetry and Jewish American Identity*. State University of New York Press (Albany, 2001); 194 pp.
Fischer, Klaus P., *The History of an Obsession: German Judeophobia and the Holocaust*. Continuum Publishing (New York, 2001); 532 pp.
Fredman, Stephen, *A Menorah for Athena: Charles Reznikoff and the Jewish Dilemmas of Objectivist Poetry*. University of Chicago Press (Chicago, 2001); 193 pp.
Gartner, Lloyd P., *History of the Jews in Modern Times*. Oxford University Press (Oxford, 2001); 468 pp.
Gross, Jan T., *Neighbors: The Destruction of the Jewish Community in Jedwabne, Poland*. Princeton University Press (Princeton, 2001); 261 pp.
Haber, Leo, *The Red Heifer*. Syracuse University Press (Syracuse, 2001); 289 pp.
Hedaya, Yael, *Housebroken*. Metropolitan Books (New York, 2001); 307 pp.
Heilman, Samuel C., *When a Jew Dies: The Ethnography of a Bereaved Son*. University of California Press (Berkeley, 2001); 271 pp.
Horn, Shifra, *The Fairest Among Women*. St. Martins Press (New York, 1998); 293 pp.
Kremer, Roberta S., (ed.), *Memory and Mastery: Primo Levi as Writer and Witness*. State University of New York Press (New York, 2001); 248 pp.
LaCapra, Dominick, *Writing History, Writing Trauma*. The Johns Hopkins University Press (Baltimore, 2001); 226 pp.
Levy, Herbert, (ed.), *Jacob Frank: The End to the Sabbataian Heresy: Translated from Polish "Frank I Frankisci Polscy, 1726–1816" by Alexandr Kraushar*. University Press of America (Lanham, 2001); 553 pp.
Liberman, Jacob, *Wisdom from an Empty Mind*. Empty Mind Publications (Sedona, 2001); 138 pp.
Littell, Franklin H., *Historical Atlas of Christianity*. Continuum Publishing Group, Inc. (New York, 2001); 440 pp.
Lucas, Eric, *The Sovereigns: A Jewish Family in the German Countryside*. Northwestern University Press (Evanston, 2001); 158 pp.
Mack, Phyllis, and Omer Bartov, (eds.), *In God's Name: Genocide and Religion in the Twentieth Century*. Berghahn Books (New York, 2001); 401 pp.
Mommsen, Hans, (ed.), *The Third Reich: Between Vision and Reality: New Perspectives on German History 1918–1945*. Berg (New York, 2001); 127 pp.
Naumov, Vladimir P., and Joshua Rubenstein, (eds.), *Stalin's Secret Pogrom: The Postwar Inquisition of the Jewish Anti-Fascist Committee*. Yale University Press (New Haven, 2001); 527 pp.
Ofrat, Gideon, *The Jewish Derrida*. Syracuse University Press (Syracuse, 2001); 201 pp.

---

* Listing here does not preclude future review.

Penslar, Derek J., *Shylock's Children: Economics and Jewish Identity in Modern Europe*. University of California Press (Berkely, 2001); 374 pp.
Politzer, Bernard, *Walachian Years: Politico-Cultural Chronicle of a Youth, 1940–1960*. Balaban Publishers (Rehovot, 2001); 226 pp.
Polliack, Meira and Colin F. Baker, (ed.), *Arabic and Judaeo-Arabic Manuscripts in the Cambridge Genizah Collections*. Cambridge University Press (Cambridge, 2001); 616 pp.
Rossi, Azariah De', *The Light of the Eyes*. Yale University Press (New Haven, 2001); 802 pp.
Roth, John K., and Carol Rittner, (eds.), *"Good News" After Auschwitz? Christian Faith within a Post-Holocaust World*. Mercer University Press (Macon, 2001); 215 pp.
Ruderman, David B., *Jewish Enlightenment*. Princeton University Press (Princeton, 2000); 291 pp.
Santner, Eric L., *On the Psychotheology of Everyday Life: Reflections on Freud and Rosenzweig*. University of Chicago Press (Chicago, 2001); 156 pp.
Satlow, Michael L., *Jewish Marriage in Antiquity*. Princeton University Press (Princeton, 2001); 431 pp.
Shapir, Yiftah, and Shai Feldman, (eds.), *The Middle East Military Balance 2000–2001*. Belfer Center for Science and International Affairs, John F. Kennedy School of Government, Harvard University (Cambridge, 2001); 425 pp.
Solomon, Lewis D., *The Jewish Tradition and Choices at the End of Life: A New Judaic Approach to Illness and Dying*. University Press of America (Lanham, 2001); 316 pp.
Stoltzfus, Nathan, and Robert Gellately, (eds.), *Social Outsiders in Nazi Germany*. Princeton University Press (Princeton, 2001); 332 pp.
Thiede, Carsten Peter, *The Dead Sea Scrolls and the Jewish Origins of Christianity*. Palgrave (New York, 2001); 256 pp.
Wellhausen, Julius, *The Pharisees and Sadducees: An Examination of Internal Jewish History*. Mercer University Press (Mercer, 2001); 115 pp.
Wright, Dale S., and Steven Heine, (eds.), *The Koan: Texts and Contexts in Zen Buddhism*. Oxford University Press (New York, 2001); 322 pp.

CONTRIBUTORS

YOEL FINKELMAN is completing a Ph.D. in the department of Jewish Thought at the Hebrew University of Jerusalem. He is writing a dissertation on the public and political function of religion in American Jewish thought.

JEFFREY HAUS received his Ph.D. from the Department of Near Eastern and Judaic Studies at Brandeis University, and is Visiting Assistant Professor of Jewish Studies at Tulane University. His most recent article, "How Much Latin Should a Rabbi Know? State Finance and Rabbinical Education in Nineteenth-Century France" appeared in *Jewish History,* Vol. 15 (Spring 2001). He is currently writing a book about the financial relationship between Jewish education and State in nineteenth-century France.

STANLEY NASH is Professor of Hebrew Literature at Hebrew Union College-Jewish Institute of Religion in New York City. He is the author of *In Search of Hebraism: Shai Hurwitz and His Polemics in the Hebrew Press* (1980); *Migvan: Studies in Honor of Jacob Kabakoff and Ben Historiyyah le-Sifrut: Studies in Honor of Isaac Brazilay* (1997); and numerous articles on Hebrew literary figures, novels, themes, and trends.

HENRY WASSERMANN is a Professor on the Staff of the Open University of Israel. He is the Editor-in-Chief of *Pinkas Hakehillot Encyclopaedia of Jewish Communities from their Foundation until after the Holocaust, Germany, Vol III, Hesse-Hesse-Nassau-Frankfort* (1992) and the author of *False Start: Jewish Studies at German Universities during the Weimar Republic* (forthcoming).

"EXQUISITE MASTERY"*

"In *Reading the Zohar*, Giller has succeeded in producing a work that will engage nonacademic readers while still making a substantial contribution to the scholarly study of Jewish mysticism." —*Choice*.

"Pinchas Giller...has an exquisite mastery of both primary and secondary materials in the study of Kabbalah in general, and Zohar in particular....As *Reading the Zohar* unfolds, the centuries of ideological accretions are slowly separated out, and the reader comes to understand how Jewish mystical ideas developed over time and what implications those concepts had inside Jewish intellectual life. Yet, for all his mastery of academic texts, Giller writes plainly and clearly."
—*The Jewish Journal of Greater Los Angeles.**

The Zohar, a massive compilation of commentaries on the Hebrew Bible, is the central Jewish mystical work. Its teachings have dominated the development of Jewish mysticism, or Kaballah. To the present day, the Zohar continues to provide the foundation of much Jewish mystical thought and practice. In this book, Pinchas Giller examines certain key sections of the Zohar and the ways in which the central doctrines of classical Kabbalah took shape around them.

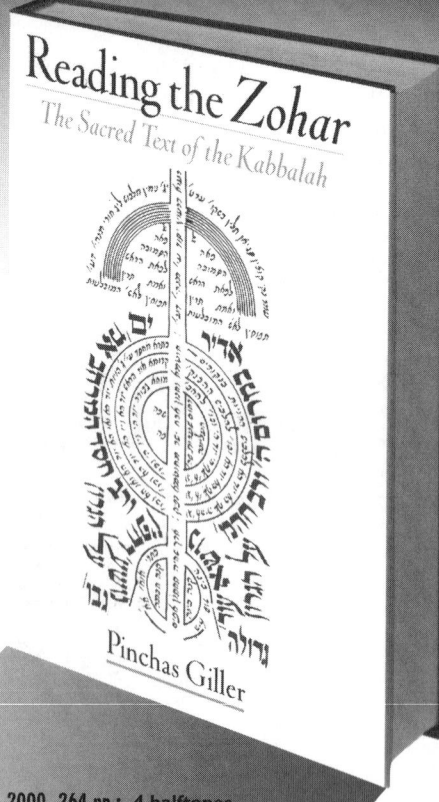

2000   264 pp.;   4 halftones & 2 line illus $65.00

Prices are subject to change and apply only in the US. To order, or for more information, please call 1-800-451-7556. In Canada, call 1-800-387-8020. Visit our website at www.oup.com

OXFORD
UNIVERSITY PRESS

JEWISH STUDIES

THE CHANGING FACES OF JESUS
GEZA VERMES
"Geza Vermes is one of the most distinguished living scholars of ancient Judaism....In Vermes Jesus has found his best Jewish interpreter."—E. P. Sanders, The *New York Review of Books*.
Maps.
Penguin Compass 336 pp.
0-14-219602-9 $15.00

WHEN I LIVED IN MODERN TIMES
A Novel
LINDA GRANT
In 1946, Evelyn Sert stands on the deck of a ship bound for Palestine and embarks on a discovery—of herself, of her heritage, and of the land that would become Israel. "A stunning accomplishment...a vivid account of an elusive piece of recent history."—*Chicago Sun-Times*. Winner of the Orange Prize for Fiction.
Plume 272 pp.
0-452-28292-6 $13.00

BLACK, WHITE, AND JEWISH
Autobiography of a Shifting Self
REBECCA WALKER
"A beautifully written meditation on the creation of a woman's sense of self. It is about being black, white, and Jewish, born in the throes of the political sixties, coming of age in the conflicted and complex eighties and nineties."—Jane Lazarre.
Riverhead 336 pp.
1-57322-907-5 $14.00

FRAGILE BRANCHES
Travels Through the Jewish Diaspora
JAMES R. ROSS
"Will become a standard work in Judaica."—*Beliefnet.com*. Through descriptions of his visits to six unusual Jewish communities—in Peru, Brazil, India, the Amazon, Israel, and Uganda—Ross offers a new perspective on ancient questions, thoughts, and rituals.
Riverhead 240 pp.
1-57322-895-8 $14.00

PENGUIN PUTNAM INC.
ACADEMIC MARKETING DEPARTMENT • 375 HUDSON ST. • NY, NY 10014-3657 • www.penguinputnam.com

Introduce your library to
Modern Judaism

OXFORD
UNIVERSITY PRESS

Editor:
Steven Katz
Boston University

Just photocopy this page, fill in the name and address, and OUP will send a free sample copy of *Modern Judaism* without obligation!

I would like to send the below named library a FREE sample copy of *Modern Judaism* without obligation.

Library

Address

City/State/Zip

Country

Return to:
Journals Marketing,
Oxford University Press,
2001 Evans Road, Cary, NC 27513
The Americas Tel: 919-677-0977 or
1-800-852-7323 (US & Canada only)
Fax: 919-677-1714
UK/Europe/Rest of World Tel:
+44 (0) 1865 267 907
Fax: +44 (0) 1865 267 485

World Wide Web:
mj.oupjournals.org

0007modjud/libr01

Raul Hilberg
Sources of Holocaust Research

The master historian of the Holocaust distills a lifetime of scholarly investigation into this indispensable analysis of the writing of Holocaust history. Drawing on a great many examples, he discusses the nature of the sources upon which factual writing about the events are based, explaining the structure, style, and content of the source materials in common use. This examination, not previously attempted, opens wide vistas and will be welcomed by all readers interested in the foundations of historical knowledge.

Ivan R. Dee, Publisher
Chicago • A Member of the Rowman & Littlefield Publishing Group
At your bookseller, or order toll-free 1-800-462-6420 with a major credit card.

To advertise in this journal, please contact:

Helen Pearson
Oxford Journals Advertising
P. O. Box 347
Abingdon, OX14 1GJ, UK
Tel/Fax: +44 (0) 1235 201 904
E-mail: helen@oxfordads.com

MODERN JUDAISM
ORDER FORM

PLEASE ENTER MY ONE-YEAR SUBSCRIPTION TO **MODERN JUDAISM**

VOLUME 22, 2002 • 3 ISSUES/YEAR • ISSN 0276-1114

___INSTITUTIONAL RATE: $121/£82 • ___INDIVIDUAL RATE: $48/£37

PLEASE NOTE £STERLING RATES APPLY IN EUROPE, US$ ELSEWHERE.

NAME: _____

ADDRESS: _____

_____

CITY/STATE/ZIP: _____

___I ENCLOSE THE CORRECT PAYMENT. (CHECK PAYABLE TO OXFORD UNIVERSITY PRESS.)

___PLEASE CHARGE MY: MASTERCARD/ VISA/ AMEX/DINERS (CIRCLE ONE)

CARD NUMBER: _____

EXPIRATION DATE: _____

SIGNATURE: _____

PLEASE RETURN YOUR COMPLETED ORDER FORM TO:

In North America
Journals Marketing
Oxford University Press
2001 Evans Road
Cary, NC 27513, USA
(800) 852-7323
or (919) 677-0977
Fax: (919) 677-1714
e-mail: jnlorders@oup-usa.org

Elsewhere
Journals Department
Oxford University Press
Great Clarendon Street
Oxford OX2 6DP, UK.
+44 (0) 1865 267907
Fax: +44 (0) 1865 267485
e-mail: jnl.orders@oup.co.uk

Stay Alert!
Stay on top of what *Modern Judaism* is publishing by signing up for its FREE e-toc service. Have the table of contents of each issue e-mailed to you prior to publication. To activate, please visit **www.mj.oupjournals.org** and click on "content alerting."

OXFORD
UNIVERSITY PRESS